Mandalas and More

Mandalas *and More*

A MEDITATIVE DRAWING AND COLORING BOOK FOR MIND, BODY, AND SPIRIT

CHER KAUFMANN

The Countryman Press
A division of W. W. Norton & Company
Independent Publishers Since 1923

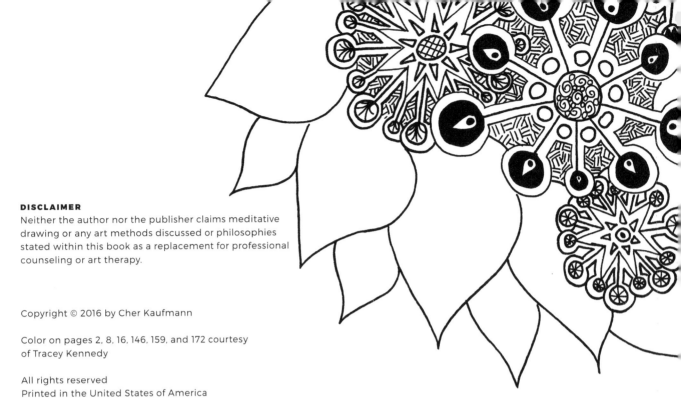

DISCLAIMER

Neither the author nor the publisher claims meditative drawing or any art methods discussed or philosophies stated within this book as a replacement for professional counseling or art therapy.

For information about permission to reproduce selections from this book, write to Permissions, The Countryman Press, 500 Fifth Avenue, New York, NY 10110

For information about special discounts for bulk purchases, please contact W. W. Norton Special Sales at specialsales@wwnorton.com or 800-233-4830

The Countryman Press
www.countrymanpress.com

A division of W. W. Norton & Company, Inc.
500 Fifth Avenue, New York, NY 10110
www.wwnorton.com

978-1-58157-344-2 (pbk.)

10 9 8 7 6 5 4 3 2 1

Special thanks to Mark Kaufmann, Tracy Vega, Ann Treistman, and all my students for their input and encouragement. Tracey Kennedy, thank you for all of your dedicated time in coloring several mandalas in the book as well as for the cover art. Mom, Dad, Don, and Mary— my personal cheerleaders—you are awesome, thank you! This book is dedicated to all artists, hidden and known. May your creative fire be seen in every stroke of your pen in ways that surprise and thrill you. It only takes the light of a small kindle to inspire awe. Be this, and glow.

Contents

Introduction

Welcome to the world of *Mandalas and More: A Meditative Drawing and Coloring Book for Mind, Body, and Spirit,* a place where creating beauty on paper is easy to learn *and* easy to do. In these pages, first-time artists can find themselves making beautiful images while more experienced doodlers can expand their artistic talents. The art of easy pattern building, or how and where to find inspiration during an average day, weaves through this book, guiding you to treasures hidden in your home, your yard, or in nature—even in what might seem the most mundane. Magic happens in simple places.

Doodles, drawings, etchings, petroglyphs, pottery, sculptures, and textiles all hold secrets to capturing the inspiration of the world line by line, loop by loop, and dot by dot. Humans have created works of art and recorded history and time through these arts, from the simple to the intricate, leaving important marks in the exterior world.

What you might not expect is what drawing can do for your interior world. Studies have shown drawing, and especially drawing that induces relaxation, not only acts as a stress reducer but uses both sides of the brain with beneficial results. In basic terms, people think of the left side of the brain as the logical one, helping to process mathematical equations, language, and factual memory, while the right side is known as the artistic one, responsible for spatial and abstract processing, such as is found in painting and music. However, this understanding is too simplistic. In actuality, while each side has its own personality

with respect to processing information, both are constantly communicating within a circuitry to cultivate a larger meaning, combining intuition and tactile input to manage personal experience.

When creating a drawing pattern and building upon it using the methods discussed here, the journey of the left side of the brain connects to something it can see and do physically, creating focus, stimulating brain function, and helping with memory as it repeats patterns in the art. The left side of the brain truly loves patterns: It works more efficiently when it knows it can count on one—like walking a straight line, a pattern is logical and efficient. Meanwhile, the right side of the brain engages in accessing creative problem solving, tapping intuition through more abstract processing. Exercises that use both sides of the body, like crawling, have shown similar results in getting both sides of the brain to interact more successfully. While the left brain becomes consciously busy with the act of focusing on a pattern, the creative or intuitive right side activates to merge with its logical other half, interweaving action and possibility.

This can have surprising results. What many artists start as "just a drawing" can evolve to inspire something unexpected in other parts of their lives. One part of life is not separate from the others. Each part is interwoven like small waves in the ocean meeting the land. And it may appear that the ocean and land are separate entities but at the moment when they touch each other, they are simply the shore.

There's a famous saying from the philosopher Lao Tzu that's often translated into English as "The journey of a thousand miles begins with a single step." However, a more literal translation is actually, "The journey of a thousand miles begins beneath one's feet." This means before you even start to take your first step, the journey begins with where you are and who you are in the present moment, for it is you, after all, who will be taking that step. Realizing this truth can have profound implications on a journey

before it is even taken, or it can serve as a revelation of how far you have come!

The chapters in this book are guideposts along a journey that may at first glance seem to be simple or even technical, but as you go you will find that the real learning is in *how* to see the hidden. Lao Tzu's place "beneath one's feet" and the journey ahead begin here, by holding this book in your hand.

Hence, I often refer to this activity as meditative drawing. The process is much more important than what is created. In the progression of allowing yourself to be with each step along the way, the mind focuses, the body relaxes, and you enter a state of enjoyment that can feel like a suspension of time where stress is reduced. Results created on paper are simply the bonus of drawing . . . and the beginning of realizing even greater potentials.

As for myself, I have always been interested in patterns and all the different ways they appear. I have an eclectic background of different professional and personal endeavors. My creative background is rooted in art, photography, music, and writing. I have studied art since I was a child, using markers and crayons or whatever we had available, until my dad introduced me to charcoal, which was my medium of choice for a while. Other kids might have had lemonade stands, but at age five I was trying to sell my drawings from my driveway at the end of a cul-de-sac in the foothills of the Arizona mountains. In college, I was hired to be the lab technician in the screen-printing, etching, and printmaking department at the community college. I assisted students with their projects and kept an eye on the lab. Then, after college, I got married, and expanded my studies by learning Reiki. I also became interested in alternative health care.

I was fascinated by the patterns in chiropractic studies as well as the diverse studies of theology and almost pursued degrees in both. I obtained professional degrees in massage therapy, became a teaching Reiki master, and studied Chinese Face Reading and many alternative healing therapies, including the Five Element theory of Chinese medicine and the basics of Ayurveda. Each of the modalities I studied simply added to my interest in details and patterns within people, the world around us, and the relationship between the two. The appreciation of knowing there is more to see and do, so often overlooked, has become increasingly important to recognize.

I am a perpetual student of patterns in people, in nature, and in the world around me. Finding treasures to share with artists and readers, young and old, is part of my journey. The place "beneath my feet" motivates me to help others see their own intuitive abilities in order to inspire wonderful lives.

—Cher Kaufmann, Inspirational Art Instructor

Best Experience

There are no rules in this style of drawing, but there are ways to get the best experience during your journey. Feel free to tear out this page, using both sides, as a personal Art Guide and perhaps to bookmark your location along the way.

1. **BREATHE.** The best way to begin anything new is to breathe, both in and out. Don't hold your breath!

2. **START WITH WHAT YOU KNOW.** Circles, triangles, ovals, squares, straight lines, curved lines, or dots—anything goes.

3. **NOTICE WHAT YOU NOTICE.** The mere act of noticing can open a world of observation in a whole new way. (Think of hubcaps and tires on vehicles—they are all circles with different designs!)

4. **BREAK IT DOWN.** How would you draw that object? Begin with the most basic, discernable shape. Often it is something as simple as an item listed in suggestion #2.

5. **SLOW DOWN.** Rushing through patterns has larger implications regarding how you use your personal vitality. Be connected to what you are doing and enjoy the drawing experience.

6. **RESPECT YOUR ART—AND OTHERS, TOO.** I teach "clean art," as in keeping your paper clean. You can actually prevent smearing pencil lines and unknowingly depositing dirt and oil onto your paper. Protect your important works of art. It is a sign of personal respect as well.

7. **EXPLORE, RESEARCH, PLAY, AND EXPAND.** Be inspired by other artists, cultural art, and everyday objects, but most of all, by the world around you. At the end of this book, there is a list of places to look for hidden wonders of inspirational patterns.

8. **TRY NEW TOOLS.** Be willing to use all pencils, pens, and papers. You don't have to wait to have that special pen or paper to get started. You have all you need with a writing utensil, an appropriate surface, and your willingness to let it flow.

Body Scan ABC

ADJUST your body and paper for comfort. How you hold your body can make a big difference in enjoyment. Tear out your page so you can easily turn the paper at the angle that best suits the process. See the special note below for tips on relaxing your physical body.

BREATHE easily and let tension go. A nice deep breath is an easy way to release any excess tension, and it helps to relax your mind. Lower your shoulders during the exhale.

CONNECT pen to paper in a soft, firm way. All the pen has to do is gently touch the paper. No need to press hard. Connect to one pattern at a time. This simple idea will keep you from doing too much at once. Less is more in this case.

WHEN YOU HOLD YOUR PEN, RELAX YOUR SHOULDERS. RELAX YOUR JAW. Let your eyebrows and your lips soften. Focus on the pattern and let everything else move away. Subtle tensions will have a way of creeping up into your thoughts and your drawing. Gently be aware of being relaxed while holding the pen and allowing the ink to put its impression on the paper, nothing forced. This will be the same approach to all your lines in this process—having fun, being relaxed, and enjoying what the pen and paper reveal along the way.

How to Use This Book

TEAR-OUT PAGES. This book has been uniquely created to take you along on the journey through each stage of drawing and coloring. Using the tear-out pages, you can easily follow the examples in the book, rotating your paper for easy drawing and coloring, allowing you to quickly develop muscle memory as you learn the patterns. Each page you tear out is designed to be removed. You will not lose any instructions once these pages leave the book, and you will have plenty of drawing room to explore!

HINT:

All pages are perforated so you can easily tear out pages and take with you to practice your skills.

Take the previous page with you for easy reference, incorporating the three steps every time you set out to draw. With time, you will automatically adjust, breathe, and connect effortlessly, which will greatly enhance your experience and merge your inner self to your outer experience.

Chapter One

Basic Techniques

"Bottomless wonders spring from simple rules which are repeated without end."
—BENOIT MANDELBROT

While studying cauliflower in the mid-1970s, mathematician Benoit Mandelbrot made an interesting observation. If you take a piece of cauliflower away from the main bunch, that piece is a replica of the larger bunch. This is different than if you take a piece of a flower away from the main flower, which leaves you with a petal, a leaf, or the stem. But cauliflower only changes in scale, not in representation! A floret of cauliflower, even if separated from an already very small floret, still resembles the original bunch.

Dr. Mandelbrot figured there had to be a mathematical equation for this type of patterning. With the use of computers, he and his team were able to develop an exact equation for reading and predicting these patterns, which Mandelbrot called fractals. Properly defined, a fractal is a natural phenomenon or a mathematical set that exhibits a repeating pattern that displays at every scale.

Through Dr. Mandelbrot's simple act of observing of a natural phenomenon, a scientific discovery was made. Intricate patterns of infinite complexity can now be mapped and harnessed for art and science, all because of one man's study of cauliflower. Imagine what secrets can be discovered when you look at the many shapes and forms in your day!

It is this idea of using self-similar patterns—very simple ones—that begins the creation of intricate drawings. As with cauliflower, basic lines can look complex when placed together. You can create magnificence by slowly building one pattern upon another like leaves in a tree. Observation, awareness, and beingness start with you.

"The journey of a thousand miles begins beneath one's feet." Lao Tzu's famous quote is often referenced to inspire movement toward the next level of learning about one's self and taking a chance, helping a traveler or a student trust in where they will be going. The same notion applies to drawing. Starting from somewhere, going to anywhere, has to begin here. "No matter where you go—there you are," is how Confucius, China's most famous philosopher and teacher, expressed this thought. Observing something small can be the inspiration toward building a masterpiece. Who knew cauliflower would have the impact it did when Dr. Mandelbrot observed it that day? Begin to open yourself to seeing your world with awe as well.

Drawing, Doodling, and Coloring Tools

Doodles and drawings can be done with anything: a ballpoint pen and a piece of scrap paper, markers and construction paper, copy paper and a pencil, or drawing paper and a good pen. It is more about the process and less about the tools. The tools facilitate learning more about yourself than you may now realize. As you go along, you will find that certain tools lend a different kind of connectivity to your drawing. And confidence has a way of expanding a budding artist's tool chest. I like to work with a variety of papers, pens, and pencils. I am certain that by the time you read this, my list will have grown and shifted because I've been experimenting with new tools. Be adventurous about what you draw with for fun and what you like to use to make your more important pieces of art (for example, a gift to a friend or family member might be done on a higher quality paper).

To get the curious artist started, here are a few brief notes about different types of drawing tools and papers.

Pens and Markers

Certain fine drawing, drafting, and technical pens have a special point called a nib. Nibs can be made of ceramic, metal, or felt. Traditional calligraphy pens and fountain pens have metal nibs that allow ink to move to the end via a reservoir and so they should be held at an angle. The technical pens I often use for teaching students have felt nibs that look similar to what you find on fine-tip markers, and one of these pens will last longest if used carefully, with the full nib tip making contact with the paper. This means drawing with the pen more upright, rather than at an angle like most of us do with regular handwriting. Drawing with a felt nib at an angle will bend it and wear it down faster.

In this book, the black ink in the sample illustrations comes from technical pens. I chose to use technical pens because they have ink that has minimal or no smell and dries quickly on the paper to reduce any accidental smearing.

Ballpoint pens and rollerball pens (which sound

Any drawing tool can create amazing results. Be inspired by all art. Even ballpoint pens can produce photo-like quality art.

like they are the same, but they aren't) are also nice to draw with, providing the one you're using doesn't clog or leak at the point. Experimentation is the best on these pens.

Gel pens have a smooth glide and come in many colors, including metallic and glittery varieties; however, they are a "wet" pen. This means that the ink they leave on the paper is slightly wet at first and can easily smear if your hand accidently makes contact with it before it has dried completely. Many people love the glide of the gel pen, but I recommend working carefully with it so as not to create any smudges. They can also be used in place of the traditional marker for coloring.

Markers are also useful for drawing. Be aware that most felt-tipped markers are not archival, meaning they will fade over time because they are dye based. If you want something long lasting, try archival pens—they are permanent because they have pigment-based ink, which will not fade.

For fun and experimentation, markers are an excellent choice, offering a large variety of colors and tip sizes. They are the easiest to play with if you want strong, saturated colors. Due to variations between different markers, many artists eventually settle on a brand they find works best for their art. Markers have broad, medium, or fine tips as well as varying levels of color saturation on the paper.

Brush-tip pens and brush-tip markers are fun to play with because you can use them to create exacting small lines with the very tip or broader marks if you angle the brush to make flattened contact with the paper. These are not to be confused with metal-nib calligraphy pens or the angle-tipped felt calligraphy markers, which are very different. Brush tips come in a variety of colors and thicknesses. I often use black brush-tip pens to color in larger areas of a design, because they have the ability to cover a large area quickly but can adapt to the smallest of corners and edges as needed.

Pencils

Pencils—colored, graphite or graphite-clay mixtures, and charcoal—are excellent for variety, shading, and experimentation. Colored pencils, like other writing instruments, possess a variety of qualities that can be helpful to distinguish among, depending on your art. If your colored pencil ever feels like the colored part has broken inside the wood casing (or if you drop your pencil on a hard surface), place the colored pencil in the sun or on a heating pad for a few minutes to warm the inside, which will connect the broken pieces together, like melting candle wax. Do not let it remain in the heat too long or it will melt all the way! Let it cool completely to harden it before sharpening or using.

ART POINT

Graphite and colored pencils are fun to use with pen and ink drawing. Further tips and hints on using graphite pencils and colored pencils are located in the Embellishing with Shading and Color *chapter.*

Pencil Sharpeners

Pencil sharpeners come in quite a variety now, offering long to short sharpening lengths, with some specifically made to sharpen just the very tip of the writing instrument to a wider sharp point without reducing much of the wooden casing. There are different sizes for thicker pencils and those with or without the holding tray for catching shavings. Artists who use pencils, colored or otherwise, often report favoring small, hand-held sharpeners that are well made, with sharp blades to help reduce oversharpening and loss of pencil. Electric sharpeners can be used if necessary, but be aware that their sharpening mechanisms do heat up and can soften colored pencils if used for many pencils in a row (not recommended). Always run a graphite pencil through your sharpener to clean and lubricate your sharpener after sharpening colored pencils. For a quick sharpened point, run the tip of the pencil across fine grit sandpaper.

Meditative Drawing is about the PROCESS, not the product. Take your time—the greatest benefit is allowing yourself to be with the process of simply drawing, whether you have 10 minutes or 2 hours. You can pick up where you left off or start anew at any time. Let the patterns show you what they can do.

Paper

Paper will make a big difference in your relationship with a pen or pencil. Certain pens and pencils work better with certain types of paper. Papers have different surface textures, and if a paper is designed specifically for art, that will be noted on the front of the package. Terms like "medium surface" or "smooth surface" will let you know the texture. The technical term for the texture is the "tooth" of the paper. Having the proper tooth for the medium you are using will help ensure that the medium adheres to the paper.

The writing medium will adhere and absorb differently depending on the relationship it has with the paper. If you like a particular pen but are confused at some point as to why it is writing differently, it might simply be the pen-to-paper relationship. Some paper easily absorbs a pen's ink and creates a bleed, spreading the ink outward to produce soft edges. The same pen can then be used on a different paper to create precise, crisp lines with no bleed on the edges. Be aware that changing a pen or the paper is changing a tool.

White paper will produce a different effect than a softer cream color and different still than black paper with a white pen or a colored paper background. Paper color is a great way to add something different to your drawing or background. Be aware, though, that papers with existing patterns on them can sometimes be too busy for what you are about to create. Soft patterns or patterns that remain on the edges can help frame your new creation nicely without overpowering your design.

Blenders

Tortillons (pronounced *tor-tee-YOHNS*) are small rolled paper tools used to soften and blend graphite pencils. Blending stumps are compressed paper sticks used to blend colored pencil marks. They are must-have tools for pencil shading and can be purchased at art stores. There are special colorless blending pencils for colored pencils (they contain the binding agents minus the pigment) and even blending tools for certain brands of markers designed to blend and mix. Brands of colored pencils often have their own blender pencils because the binders will be the same as the ones in the colored pencils.

ART POINT

It is helpful for beginners to simply find paper marked "Drawing Paper" at an art or hobby store to start. Pastel and charcoal artists require a much wider tooth surface to grab the medium.

Burnishers

Burnishers are objects that are usually equally as hard or harder than the medium in which you are working. Burnishers are meant to blend in a more complete way than blending sticks. Burnishers combine all the layers of the medium, smoothing them and melding them together purposefully, removing any rough elements and leaving behind a polished shine. Burnishing an object does not have to result in a shine, but it certainly smooths out imperfections or grainy appearances. Burnishing can be accomplished with a variety of objects designed specifically to bring out the shine of the medium (say on the lips of a portrait or the skin of an apple). Burnishers for colored pencils can be found at craft supply stores and look like colored pencils themselves. Tips and hints on burnishing can be found in Chapter Five where use of color is discussed. For example, gel pens can give the impression of a burnished shine if used selectively.

If in doubt, keep a sample sheet of each kind of paper you work with to try your different pens on. Experimenting with different pen/paper relationships and finding out what works for your style is part of the fun of drawing and coloring. For instance, I discovered a great relationship between a certain white pen and a specific kind of black paper. And the moment I switched to a harder card stock paper that was on sale, the pen refused to produce the same amazing results. If I had started with the card stock, I might have thought the pen was not very good.

Optional Tools

Rulers, compasses, and protractors are fabulous tools for making exact spacing, perfectly straight lines, and circular curves. However, I encourage you to start drawing *without* those tools as you learn to create fantastic expressions with line drawings. Perfection is something found not just in the pristine aspects of an artist's line but also in its imperfect, wavering aspects—just as it appears in nature.

Sometimes artists become dependent on a tool and never really explore or develop the skill of drawing because they use the tool all the time. A straight line can be drawn without a ruler if you give yourself a chance to play with it, to practice trusting and training your hand-eye coordination. Conversely, if you're looking for a particular shape or need a specific guide to help you begin, my advice is to get creative with your tools. Don't have a compass? Put a bowl, plate, or glass facedown on a sheet of paper and trace a circle to get yourself started!

In This Book

Drawings in this book were created without the use of rulers, compasses, protractors, or erasers (the only exception is in the *Meditative Mandalas* chapter, which uses a grid). As you'll see, sometimes I traced a dish or glass to create an interesting mandala frame or starter shape, and I have been known to get creative, tracing cookie cutters to use as beginner templates for teaching purposes and personal play. I draw all templates with pen. Designs here were *not* sketched with pencil and erased later. Trust that you can do it and you'll be amazed at what appears. The color you see throughout is mostly colored pencil, and shading in the ink drawings was done with graphite pencil and smoothed with a tortillon.

Get creative! I would rather have you drawing than waiting for any special tools. Start with what you have and build from there. Remember, you can draw, and virtually with anything—you do not have to have anything special to get started!

Start with what you know

**Circles, triangles, ovals, squares, straight lines,
curved lines, or dots—anything goes.**

Use shapes to create patterns. This will help you build confidence and soon new shapes and patterns will appear less intimidating, and it might even look like fun to try a more challenging style. You might find yourself trying to make something complicated right away to make it look fancy. But don't rush—your drawings will look fancy soon enough. Build confidence by starting with what you know and move up from there. Confidence in small things can help give you confidence in big things.

In Japan there is a concept called wabi-sabi. It originated in tea ceremonies when everything had to be about absolute perfection; golden spoons and pristine presentations. Then a movement began that changed everything. The Japanese started to use worn wooden spoons and nostalgic presentations—a far cry from the typical idea of "pristine." Wabi-sabi is about seeing perfection in the imperfect. In Japan, broken clay pottery, normally thrown away, can be mended with gold. This visibly mended brokenness shows this clay pottery has had experience and is now valued for that. Wabi-sabi is seeing a story through the lines of experience. In this way, be willing to see the perfection of using what you have and what you know to create amazing, unique works of art.

Circles

When beginning any drawing I like to introduce the most basic, most used, and least intimidating form: the circle. Circles are mysterious and hold the secret of life. The cycle of life moves in an ever-constant rotation that never really ends. The cycle of life continues even as the end merges with the beginning, making it whole. Circles hold a soft impression while holding a strong presence. Chinese Face Reading teaches that we intuitively respond to soft curves differently than hard edges. It has been documented that micro facial expressions are subtle physical and psychological responses mirroring what we see. When viewing soft curves, we soften our responses; when viewing hard edges, our response systems tend to reflect rigidity or absoluteness. Both are valid responses, but when it comes to finding peaceful and relaxed spaces, softer edges can help support this effect. Hence, circles are important in human connectivity and the curves help bring us "back around" again. They are a perfect place to begin drawing.

Each step you take along the journey as you draw will have a way of lending awareness to much more than this simple circle. But it is here that we begin to take notice of much more around us.

When drawing a circle, the starting and ending position are important. Making contact by putting the pen to the paper is a very important step. It is a contact that creates the relationship to the shape you are about to draw.

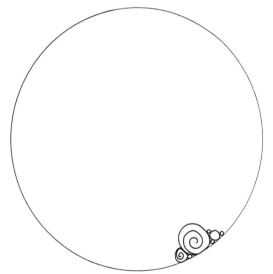

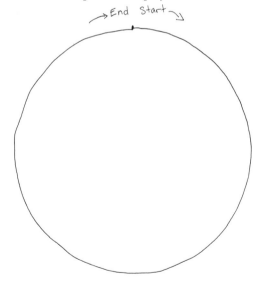

Pressing too hard into the paper or gripping the pen with tightened fingers will create strain after a while. Relax.

On the previous page I show a circle with a complete connection from the start to the end position. My pen moved in a steady, slow, continuous, connected motion on the paper the entire time all the way around to the place where I first started. While this might seem silly and overly slow, it is so important to just "be" with whatever pattern you are creating. Calligraphists and master penmen know this to be true. It is the same place from which a rider connects to the horse or a surfer unifies with the wave or the skier with the snow. Think of this magical place as akin to when a dancer or musician has fully felt the meaning of a piece of music. They are linked, intertwined, one working with the other in unison, rather than one trying to control the other. Grip-

ping the pen harder does not make a better circle, but it does tire out your hand faster! You can connect with a circle by allowing the pen to be your instrument of your motion by way of a relaxed, comfortable hold.

Even if your circle is drawn with imperfections, the connectivity between the start and end points is what will help make it a shape you can identify with. The perfection of a circle is less important than the mindfulness put toward creating it. Even a shaky hand can create lovely circles if the circle is complete in the pen to paper contact. This circle is less about the absolute pristineness of the shape and so much more about how your pen moves across the paper.

If you rush a circle, drawing fast or distractedly, it can appear more like the numbers six or nine, or like a squiggle, or sometimes like a spiral getting started. Drawing circles with open spaces left between the start and end points can give the impression of rushed drawing overall, of just wanting to "get it done." If you want your circles to really look like circles, connect the start and end points.

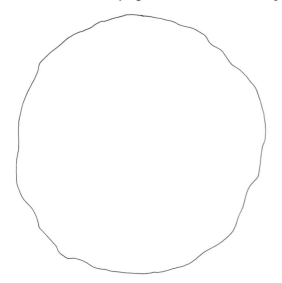

This exercise is much more than drawing circles. It's about slowing down, learning to be with a pattern, and noticing what you notice about the motion as you practice holding the pen with ease. You can also experiment with coloring in the areas around the circles as an easy way to make them stand out!

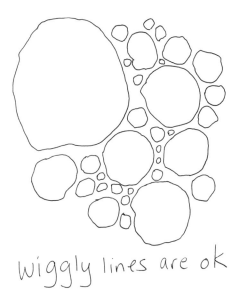

wiggly lines are ok

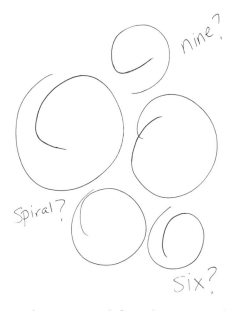

nine?

Spiral?

six?

Drawing in this way is like training a muscle to learn any new skill—it is a whole body experience. Be aware of your posture as you practice holding your pen with ease. Being aware of how your body feels when you draw will help train you to repeat shapes and patterns from muscle memory. You won't have to force them to look a certain way.

Take a moment to draw a few circles on a practice page. Relax, breathe, and enjoy. Go slow, connect the pen to the paper, and let the ink glide to create the image. Take your time. They don't have to look perfectly round—just let the start and end points connect easily. Your circle will appear before you know it. You'll feel it. Your muscles will create a memory of

the circular motion and, from then on, your body will know how to draw circles.

ART POINT

If you are using a technical pen with a nib (see "Drawing, Doodling, and Coloring Tools"), draw with your pen more upright rather than at an angle. This might slow you down a little at first, especially if you are not used to it, but with practice, your pen will last longer, you will create crisp lines, and you will provide yourself time to be with the pattern.

TEAR PLAY OUT →

MANDALAS AND MORE

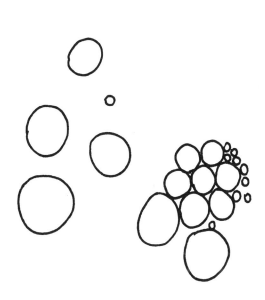

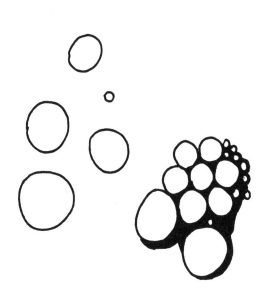

Triangles, Squares, and Rectangles

Mindful connections also apply to triangles and squares. I recommend drawing each line of the triangle or square separately until you get a nice feel of the power of a single line (briefly lift the pen after each line). Drawing three distinct lines to make a triangle or four lines for a square or rectangle will feel different than the single continuous stroke of a circle, but this will help later with more complex patterns. Relax, hold the pen firmly but gently—no gripping.

Each of the circles, triangles, and squares can be used in different proportions. The size can create space to work within or fill space that already exists. It depends on what effect you are trying to create. Take a moment to practice triangles, squares, and rectangles using the same relaxed techniques we used for circles, being mindful not to rush.

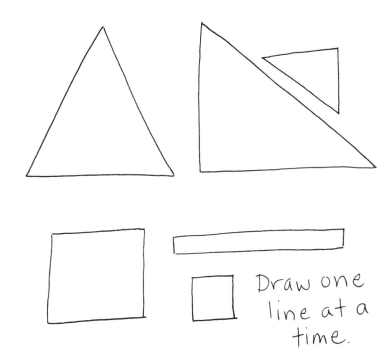

Draw one line at a time.

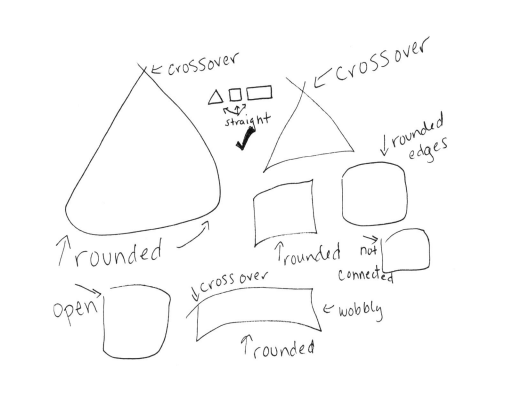

Spirals

A spiral is a gentle way of creating a variation of something familiar while adding diversity to your image. Begin spirals by making the curve of a circle and then keep your pen in motion, slowly moving inward. Or you can begin from the center and go outward, carefully closing the last rotation to the edge, creating a circle shape. You can keep a spiral open as well. Variations of spirals have been used in every culture around the world. Some appear tighter or looser in the center and some are more squared, rather than circular (see *Pattern Library*).

Combining circles and spirals is one way to add texture and filling a space with variety, especially if the sizes change too.

Draw a combination of circles and spirals of different sizes. Use a relaxed motion, open your mind, and soften your muscles as your pen moves in the circular direction. This will help you connect to the pattern itself, which might inspire your next pattern. Be open to what comes to you in this quiet space.

Body Scan ABC

ADJUST your body and paper for comfort.

BREATHE easily and let tension go.

CONNECT pen to paper in a soft, firm way. Show confidence in your lines.

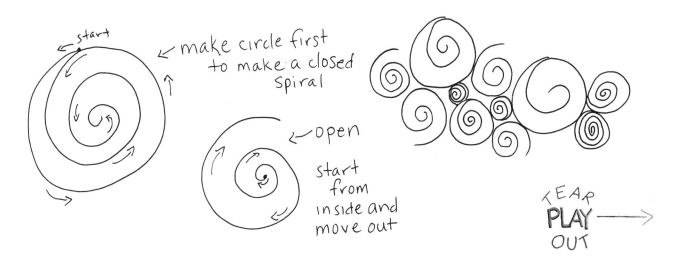

← start

← make circle first to make a closed spiral

← open

start from inside and move out

TEAR
PLAY ⟶
OUT

MANDALAS AND MORE

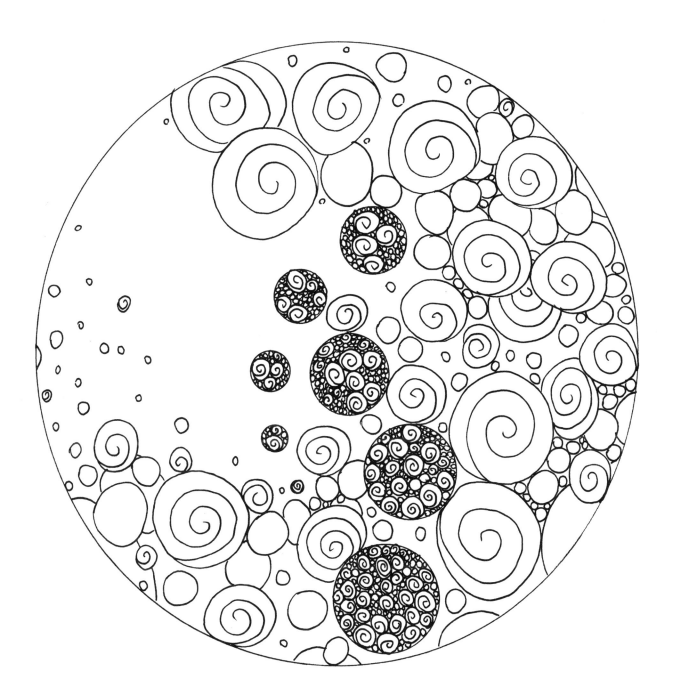

Lollipops and Balloons

Connecting a simple line to a circle can look a lot like a lollipop, or a balloon on a string. The line can be straight or curved, and the circle can be large or small.

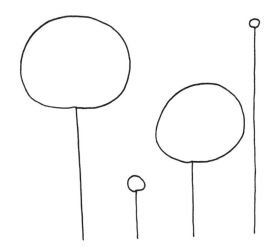 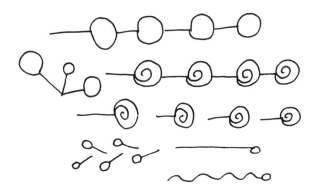

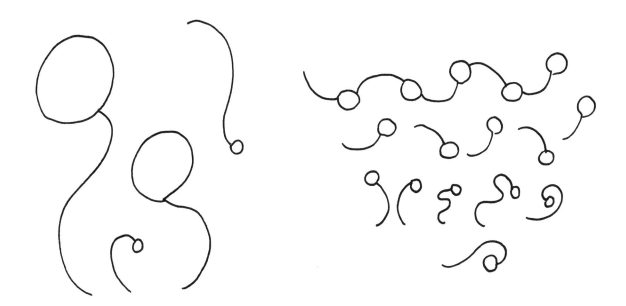

Straight Lines

Let's take a closer look at lines. Making straight lines requires a mindfulness similar to the one used when making a circle. How connected the pen is to the paper and how connected the artist is to the process of creating the line will make a difference in what it looks like. A slash will produce a hurried effect, implying a rushed energy, which is counter to the effect of relaxed drawing (unless your intention is to show movement, and then perhaps a fast line is appropriate). Be aware of the tip of the pen as it begins a line and when it ends a line—it should connect with the paper all the way across, from start to finish. Imagine the lines on pavement on a major street or highway. Lines that are clearly painted are easier to see and follow. Lines that are faded or worn over time do not have the same presence as the newly painted lines. Fast lines that prematurely lift the pen will produce a faded-out effect. Pushing off at the end of the line will produce a small ink-ball imprint.

Watch for the closure a line creates when it comes in contact with an existing line on the page. With this method of drawing, lifting the pen when it comes in contact with another line will create a cleaner, more connected drawing. Crossing over existing lines can be used with intention in some cases, but to create mindfulness in drawing and attention to detail, go up to the line, but do not cross over.

ART POINT

Line to line connection (not crossing over) helps with pattern recognition and hand-eye coordination. When you are unaware of other lines on the pages, you will run over them accidentally. There are times when lines cross over each other, intentionally, with purpose. That is a different approach. Knowing the difference can help with discovering being somewhere, with intention, and with knowing when to have the freedom of being boundless.

↳ confident line

clean connection

ink ball from "push-off"

cross over (avoid)

← faded end

← slash

←strong start

Numbers, Letters, and More

The alphabet and numbers of any language are symbols of lines that can also be used in art. I once gave a presentation at a local library for both children and adults. For part of the presentation, I asked the library to provide pens and paper for drawing designs. One of the children showed me her drawing of an ornate circular image with each layer as a different pattern. She drew with tiny, thin lines and it was not until she pointed out one of her layers that I saw her creativity at play. She said, "I didn't know what to draw so I drew numbers." And throughout that whole layer were numbers, starting with 1, 2, 3, and so on, and though the value of the number increased as she worked around the circle, the length of her lines stayed the same. It was a wonderful way to see how any line can be used to give designs a personal touch and a hint of imagination. The same thing can be done with punctuation marks! Try playing with exclamation marks, commas, periods, or question marks as your design pattern! On page 42, see what amazing things come from a simple stick figure.

ABC abc 123 123
abc 123

_ - . , ; ? ! ( ) / \ " " ' [ ] { } ~

Can you find......?

m f ;
b h B
d ! v
A :
c >
+ /
x |

TEAR
PLAY ⟶
OUT

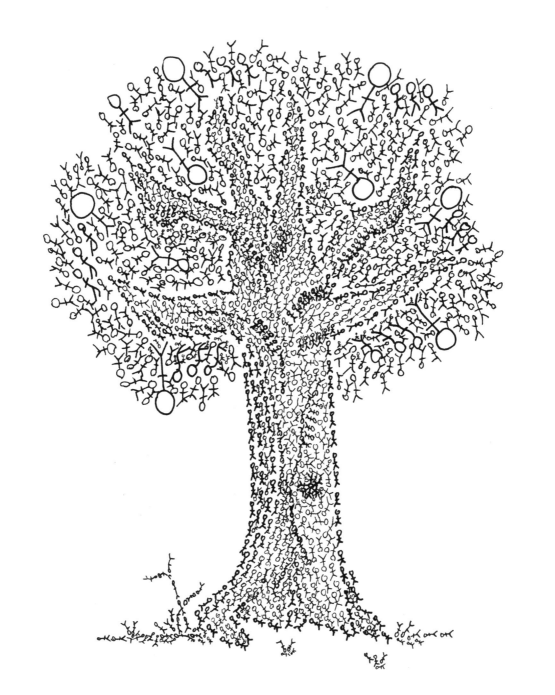

Petals and Leaves

Let's continue pattern building with leaves or petal shapes. The shapes of leaves and petals can be simple—small and rounded. Or large and rounded, or plain and pointed. Leaves come in so many amazing shapes and sizes, depending on which plant family they belong to, how close to the equator they grow, how high in altitude they climb, and whether they are water-saturated tropical plants or sparse desert cactus. For our purpose here, we will explore two basic shapes that can be altered with practice.

Placing small groups of the same shape is an easy way of adding complexity to something very simple. Take your time when drawing them. Sometimes, you might think, "I know what I'm doing," and begin to speed up. That is not what this is about. Slowing down is the trick to creating beautiful and meaningful designs. In my classes, I can always tell when someone has decided to look for the end of the pattern rather than being with the strokes of each motion.

This happens because the left side of the brain begins to recognize the pattern, and shifts into action mode to find the most efficient way to complete the process in order to move onto the next thing. This keeps the brain active and moving quickly in processing. This is how athletes practice. They speed up the process to create faster muscle reactions and quicker responses. The same goes for any skill that requires muscle control—it is about connection from mind to body in a way that moves together at the same time for what is needed.

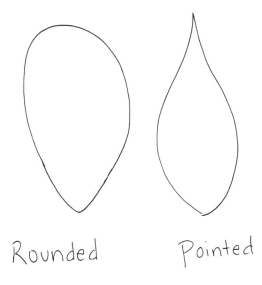

Rounded   Pointed

Now you that you know this, be aware of it and take your time in drawing the leaf shape in the same manner as you have learned to draw the circle. Connect the pen to the stroke all the way around to the starting point.

A leaf or petal shape can be reproduced inside or outside of the original shape to create different effects and to build upon your pattern. You are rendering the design to create a smaller or larger similar shape.

Keep in mind, the pattern will be very different if you "float" the petal shape in the middle, in the example, or if you connect your petal to the bottom of the shape. How you mimic the shape can really change the overall image.

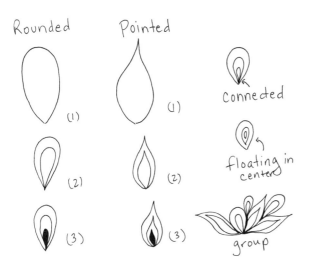

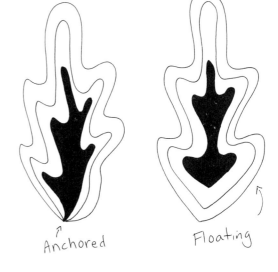

Try drawing some petal shapes. Also, experiment with different shapes.

Here are some fun ways to play with petals or leaves.

What happens if you play with putting some different shaped leaves or petals together? There is no right or wrong. Be curious about the jumble of different shapes together. Your drawing ultimately does not have to look like anything, but it can be fun to create an instant jungle or exotic floral arrangement. Your picture does not have to match mine! Use it for inspiration.

Draw one shape at a time, completely. Concentrate on not rushing in your mind to the next shape—just let the current shape develop fully and then see what shape comes to you next. Be playful, have fun. Maybe even color in some shapes with your pen.

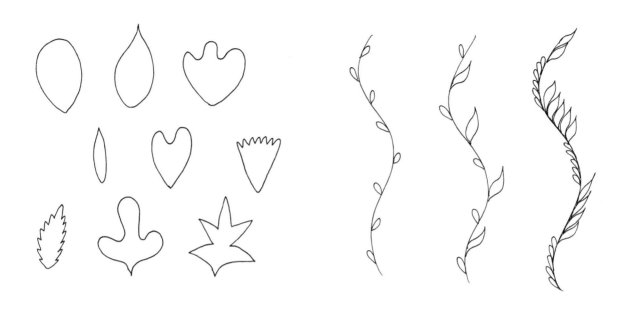

Combining Shapes and Patterns

Remember back in kindergarten when we learned that blue plus yellow makes green? Or blue plus red makes purple? And how those colors could look differently depending on how much blue was part of the mix in either equation? The same thing happens with patterns. It is as simple as adding two patterns together to begin building something interesting.

Body Scan ABC

ADJUST your body and paper for comfort.

BREATHE easily and let tension go.

CONNECT pen to paper in a soft, firm way.

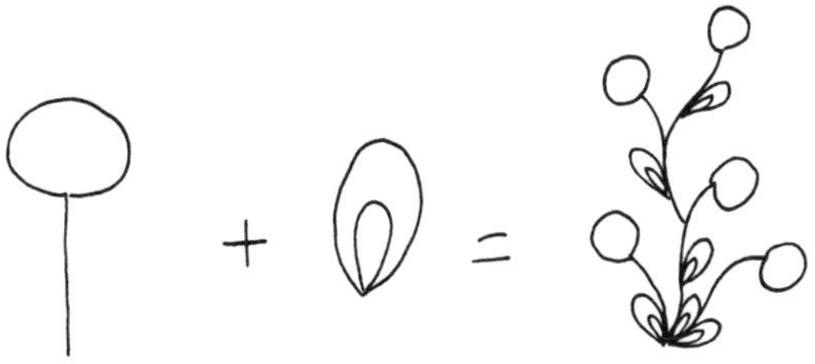

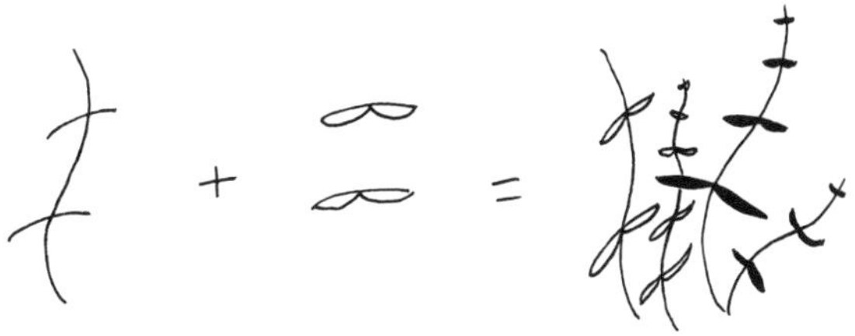

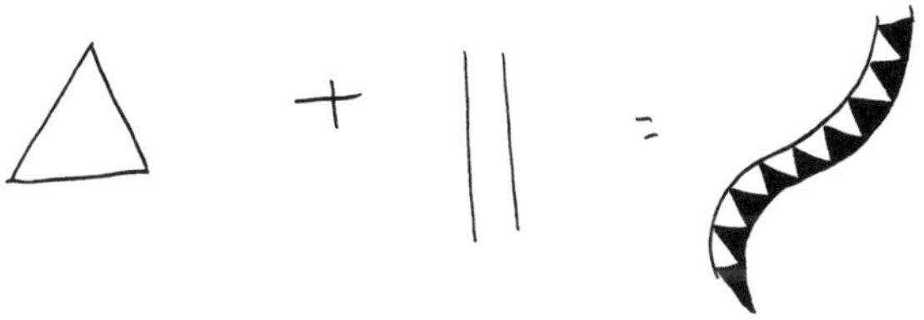

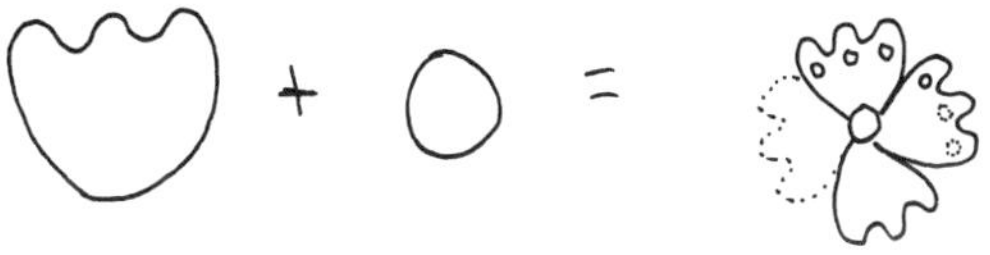

Using the petal shapes, let's take a look at how small changes can make big impacts.

Start with one pattern

Add patterns one at a time

Add pattern then begin details

Notice the difference between inking in part of a petal or drawing in small lines. Doing one detail at a time allows you to see the evolution as a whole unit. Avoid over detailing in a small area to avoid confusion if you plan on replicating the pattern.

Black

Line Design

one pattern at a time

Avoid filling one space at once

Once you learn a pattern, you can always alter it. Using a partial pattern or only doing half of a pattern is an easy way to create a whole new way to approach some-thing. There are many possibilities and roads to travel on with your pen and paper!

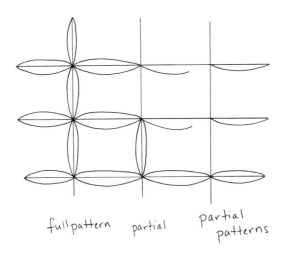

full pattern   partial   partial patterns

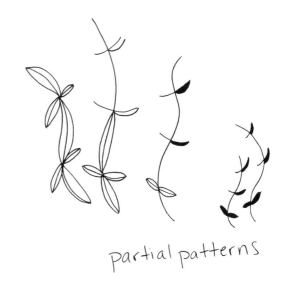

partial patterns

Shapes and Patterns

To build patterns on your page, observe patterns in nature, textures on clothing, designs on tissue boxes, how ripples in water move, and how shadows produce shapes. Tapestries, line drawings, and other artwork can inspire a new designs. Food in the kitchen is a great inspiration in the many shapes and colors that are produced to feed not only your body and mind, but also your creativity by observation. Cut open an onion, leek, or purple cabbage and layers will appear, showing possibilities to play with.

Noticing the most basic shapes in a design you see can help you create a similar design on your paper.

Continue to open your awareness to shapes and patterns, and you will learn how to connect with the process of creating them.

Let's start placing together what you know. Draw circles and lines or triangles with circles in any combination. Add ovals, spirals, and/or diamonds (draw these the same as triangles, one line at a time at first). Play with size differences for variety. Draw slowly, let the pen connect with the paper and glide across, and do not force the motion—relax.

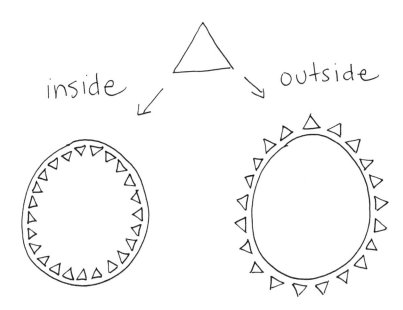

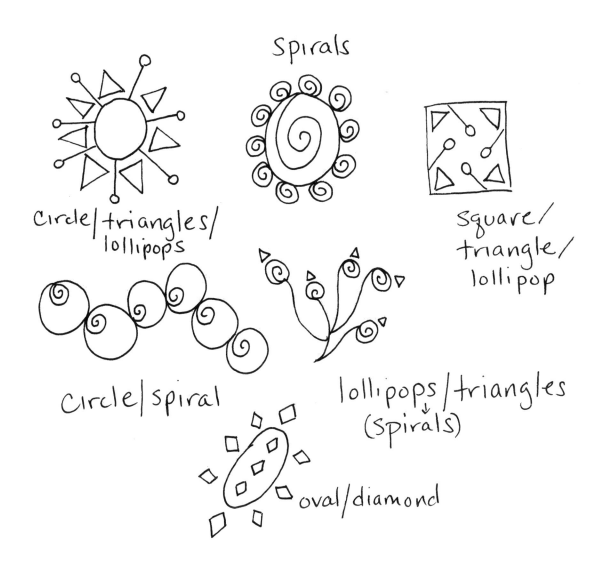

Spirals

Circle/triangles/
lollipops

Square/
triangle/
lollipop

Circle/spiral

lollipops/triangles
(spirals)

oval/diamond

Outlining

Let's talk about outlining. Outlining is when you trace around the outer edges of an existing shape. Think of drawing a rainbow, for example. One line is drawn with the second line following the same contour of the original line. Done several times, layers of the image appear like a rainbow. This same technique can be used with any shape and can vary from sharp pointed lines to soft rounded strokes. You can outline a shape exactly, or you can move outward and create an outline that's larger than the original shape. Practice outlining these starter shapes and see how it expands the image quickly!

ART POINT

Outlines create a space in which you can do anything. Fill this outlined space in, leave it blank, add a pattern, or shade it. Any space created can be designed or left alone. Outlining is the easiest and fastest way to expand your image!

original shape

follow shape outline

Rounded outline

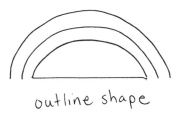

outline shape

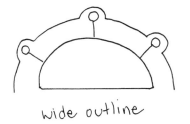

wide outline

loose outline

- original shape
- outline

- original shape
- outline
- triangles – 1ˢᵗ layer (▲)
- straight lines – 3ʳᵈ layer (|||)

- original shape
- exact outline

- original shape
- exact outline
- Build off outline (φ)

- original shape
- outline – rounded

- original shape
- outline – rounded
- triangles on top of (∆) outline
- Build off of outline (β)

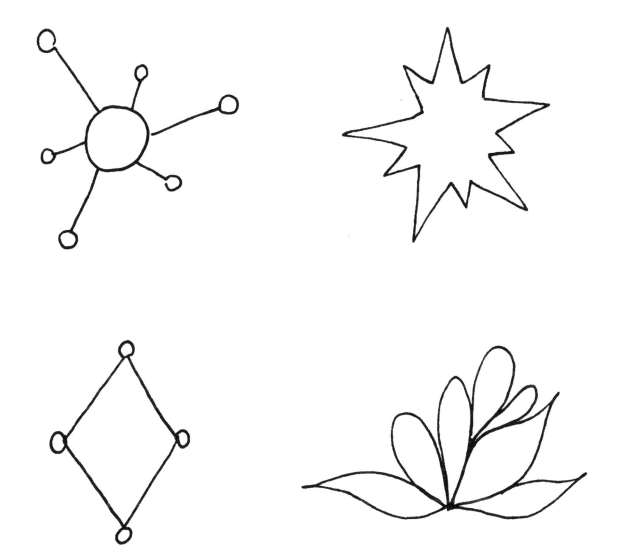

Dots

Adding dot patterns is another way to put magic and mystery into a design. Experiement with large and small dots to see the impact they have on your drawing, plus it's fun too! Add some dots to these practice patterns.

Curvy Lines

There are a lot of ways to create whimsy in your drawings, such as with soft, wavy, inky curls branching off a pattern. I like to think of the wind blowing in someone's hair or seeing young vine tendrils reaching out into the air for someplace to grab onto as they grow—something unexpected creating a quirkiness in the familiar.

Drawing lines with a soft curve can be playful and unexpected depending on where they are coming from. These special lines have no rules and can orient from the top, the side, or the bottom of the picture, or from a place among the existing patterns.

On the next page, practice your dots and curvy lines.

TEAR
PLAY ⟶
OUT

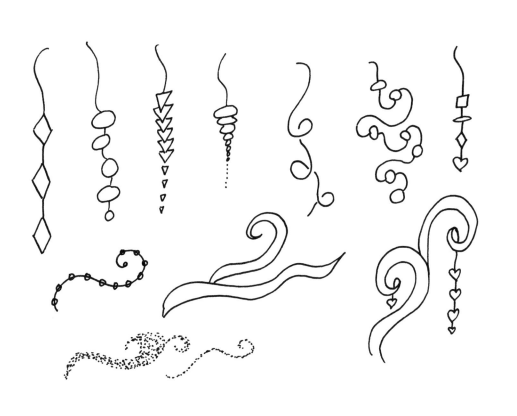

Stipple

To stipple is to create an image or impression of a design with the use of small dots only. You never let your pen glide across the paper to make a line, but rather tap the tip of the pen to the paper in a measured way. Let your pen "dot" the paper. This technique takes patience as the pen will need to create many, many small dots of approximately the same size. The amount of dots in an area, and how closely they have been put together, will create different gradations of light and dark. Practice doing regular dots all by themselves. Adjust your pressure to see how your pen marks the paper. Vary with light and firm contact. Can you draw an image from just dots on the blank page? Remember, it's okay to start with simple shapes.

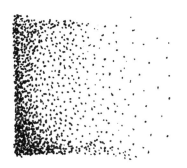

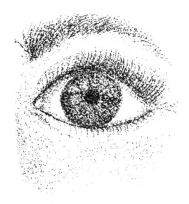

Here I use stippling to create shadows or patterns within an existing image. Try it yourself on the opposite page.

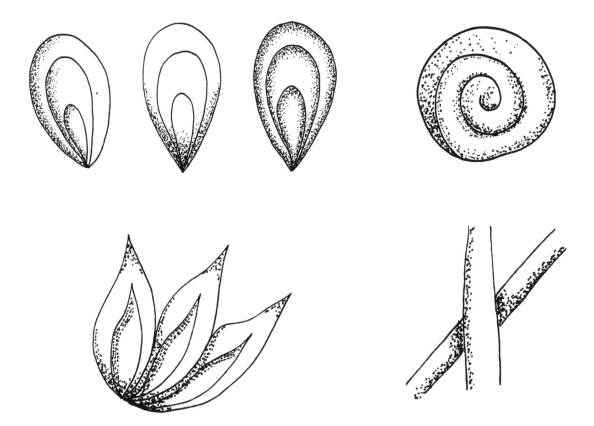

MANDALAS AND MORE

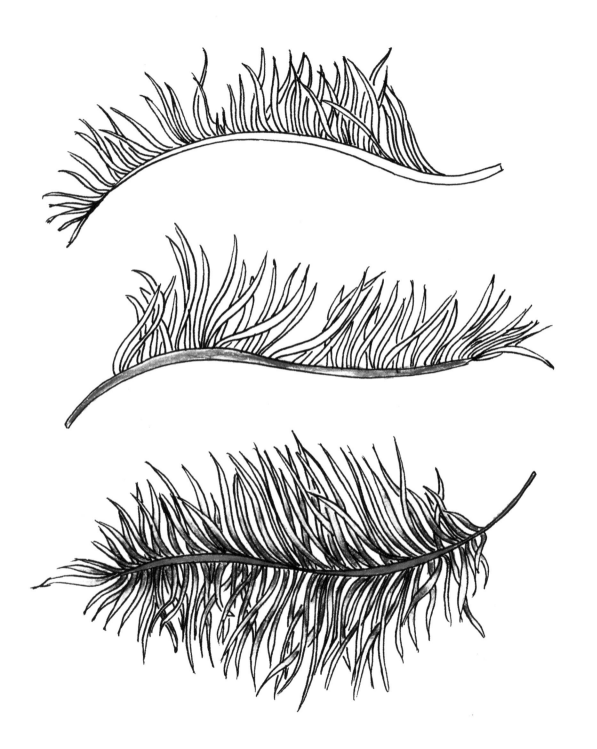

Feathers and Whispies

Here are two examples for those who like a fanciful feather or whispy lines. This is the only time where I recommend swift movements. Feathers are whispy and, well, they must be drawn that way! I start with a soft squiggle or curved line and make contact with the shaft of the feather with my pen and move away in a gentle quick movement. Place your pen strokes close together to make it more realistic. And every once in a while toss in a random line in another direction to add to the realism.

The second way is to draw open feather barbs that can be designed or colored in, by drawing two parallel lines that taper together at the tip. Draw one set of lines and have the next set appear to whisp underneath it by lifting your pen as soon as you come in contact with the existing feather barb.

This type of line play can enhance organic drawings, too!

Grass blades, for instance, can also be drawn in this way.

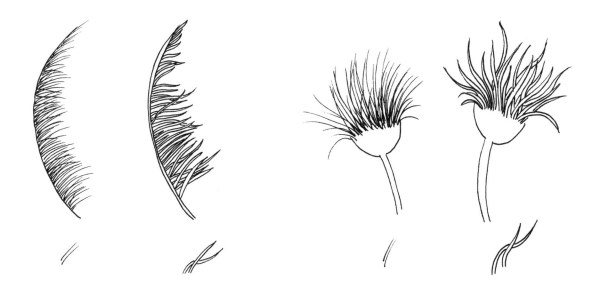

Transitions

Transition are used to fill in the space and add interest to the design without distracting from the main pattern.

Or they can be a way of filling a space with texture. Think of the grout between ceramic tiles. The color of the grout is actually an overlooked but important part of proper tile installation. If you choose the wrong color grout, it can take away from the beauty of the tile pattern. Grout, as silly as it sounds, is often a silent support, gently guiding your eyes to follow the colors and designs of the tile. Now you will never look at tile and grout the same way again. This is an important awareness: how to see, what to notice—it all counts!

Texture building for your background can be a fun way to introduce patterns that blend in but are actually interesting all by themselves. Take, for instance, the basic cardinal directions. The four directions of north, south, east, and west represent not only navigational direction but in some cultures can determine which way the front door faces for the most auspicious use of daylight and heat from the sun. Further, some studies—like Feng Shui, the study of the relationship of the environment and its inhabitants—will recommend which direction your desk should face to create the best work environment, or the best direction for the bed to be for potentially better sleep.

In drawing, the four directions can be translated to four lines: horizontal (west to east), vertical (north to south), and two diagonals (northeast to southwest and northwest to southeast). You can use all four of these lines to create an easy texture. (When I draw them, I like to move my pen and count in my head "one, two, three," and then change direction, "one, two, three," etcetera.) Notice how the look changes if the lines are close together or have a lot of space between them.

Using two of the four directions can easily produce a basket-weave pattern, which has been around for thousands of years in textiles both in actual basket-making and in other types of designs, such as stone, tile, and wood. This natural direction change also offers a variation of pattern building as shown before.

If you want to get creative with these lines, try curving them a little bit so they look like parentheses and umbrella turned up and then down. Again, spacing can change the appearance as well.

Any line can create a shape to build with. Here are a few examples of lines that can be used for pattern building and texture between patterns.

Use simple lines from the four directions: verticle, horizontal, diagonal forward, and diagonal back.

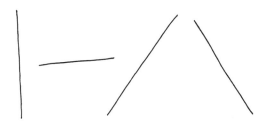

farther apart

closer together

Round your lines like parentheses or convex or con-cave for a very different result and use combinations of these lines to see what new design you can create.

TEAR PLAY OUT ⟶

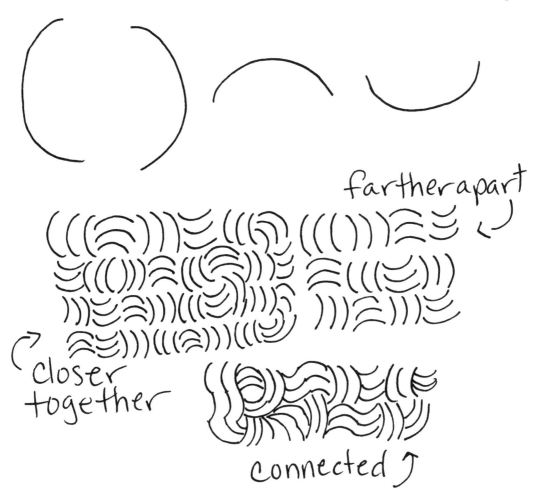

fartherapart

closer together

connected ↰

MMΞSᵕ

—/|\O

⌒∪)(

wwwww

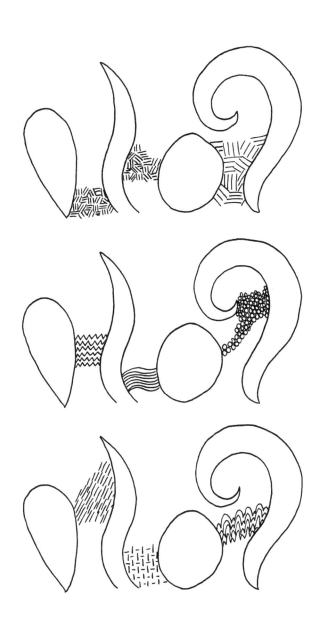

Divots

Divots between patterns—like between two circles for instance, or where one pattern meets a secondary pattern—are a great place to create something unexpected and imaginative. Use the following practice pages to play with adding whimsy, leaves, or any other pattern you're curious about. You can also ink in small areas for subtle changes or try a new texture line pattern.

Divots

TEAR
PLAY ⟶
OUT

Congratulations!

You have practiced holding our pen in a relaxed way, learned how to create patterns, and have probably begun to notice arrangements all around you with more observant eyes. Moreover, you may have started adding them to your practice pages. I have created a series of projects to help you build designs from the basics to organic to just for fun! After each project there are open practice pages designated for that project. Feel free to reference your Body Scan ABC page any time. Let's begin!

Note: At the end of every project is a tear out page for you to use to try the project. Read through the instructions first, then go back and put your pen or pencil to paper. Have fun!

Chapter Two

Freehand Pattern Building

"Every tree and plant in the meadow seemed to be dancing, those which average eyes would see as fixed and still."

—RUMI

Each tree, flower, and herb begins with a simple seed. As they grow, each is nourished from the vitality of small doses of sunshine, water, and air. The final shape of what a single seed produces can be a bit of a mystery, as it depends on the environment surrounding and sustaining the growth. As it gently waves from a buzzing bee tickling the petals or perhaps a soft breeze, each plant breathes its own life force containing colors, fragrance, and oxygen. By using the skills you learn in this book, you will no longer see from the "average eyes" Rumi refers to, but rather, from a keen eye that will spot the dance of a design by observing a pattern with renewed interest, in much the same way Rumi viewed a meadow.

In college, we learned woodblock printing. To make a print, we carved out an image on the surface of a flat piece of pine, then applied ink to the wood and printed the image to paper. Before carving, I studied the wood grain for a time, knowing that the grain had something interesting about it. Then I saw it. I saw the figure of a giant in the wood grain's natural design. It was swirled in just the right way so it looked like the giant was looking down at a tiny door at the base of a tall tree. I titled it "Invitation to Dinner." A whole story emerged through just observing the wood grain.

There can be a wonderful and liberating freedom in learning to draw from a freehanded approach. Line by line and loop by loop, you build your own designs in your distinct style. In this chapter, I will guide you in the different ways you might approach starting a freehand design from the blank page.

Where you decide to begin your visual storytelling is up to you. For some artists, the center of the paper can be the most comfortable place to start, as it allows for growth on all sides. Then there are those who draw from the corners. They may be a little shy and need the edge of the paper, like a roller skater's first time out on the rink, holding onto the wall. Just to one side of the center is another option. Either way, beginning anywhere is beginning somewhere. Just like Confucius said, "No matter where you go—there you are."

Combination Flower

This project uses only four patterns: circle, petal, circle row, triangle, and one inked-in suggestion. After completing the project, try it again with slight variations, like a rounded petal or a diamond center, to see what else you can create. Or maybe continue to add more petals. Enjoy!

Here's a very simple step-by-step on building the beginnings of a larger design.

STEP 1

Start with the small circle.

STEP 2

Add some petals, as many as you want. I kept it simple and did four. Rotate your paper to make drawing each petal super easy for you.

STEP 3

Add a series of small circles to the left side only of each petal, turning your paper as necessary to create muscle memory of the *feeling* of making the small circles.

STEP 4

Add small triangles in the center circle. Turn your paper to ensure consistency in your triangles. I made my triangles "float" in the center, not touching the circle.

STEP 5

Color in the area around your triangles for a dramatic center effect.

STEP 6

What do you want to do with the right side of the petal? If you choose to add a simple design, make sure you do that one design all the way around your image <u>before</u> you add any additional designs. This step (adding one pattern at a time) will become very important as we go into more detailed drawings. If you add too many patterns to a single petal, you can get confused as you go around the flower. Make each pattern count. Let the pattern show you what it looks like in its entirety before you add another layer!

MANDALAS AND MORE

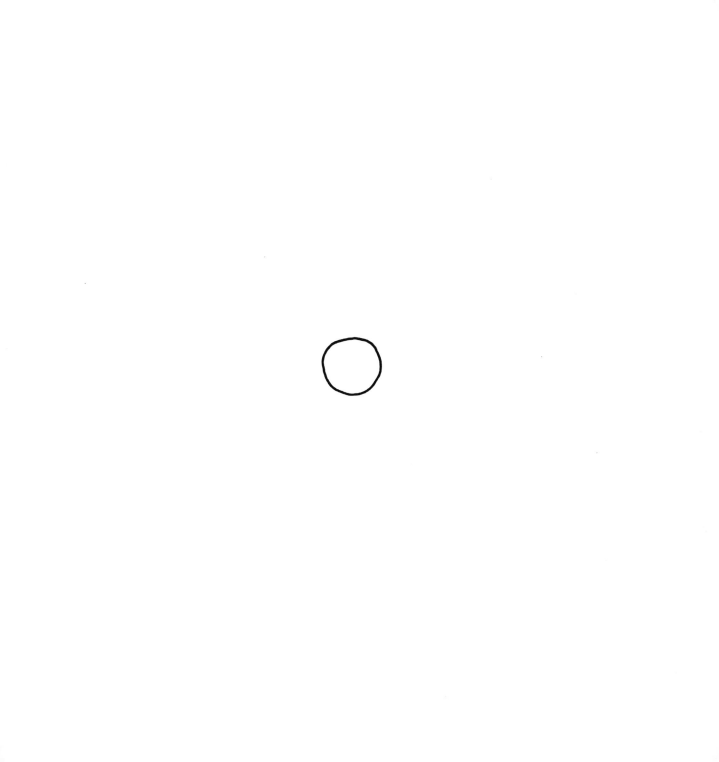

Puzzle Piece

One of the unusual patterns I teach that creates all kinds of possibilities for even more shapes and patterns inside and outside of the frame is the Puzzle Piece Pattern (PPP). This pattern works just like puzzles that have shapes that fit within each other. Sometimes, our brains want to make them a certain shape. For those of you who find yourself in this groove, you might find this a bit of a challenge at first. Think of this as something you're doing just for fun, and watch yourself create beautiful results as you let go into the shapes themselves.

FIRST LINE
FOLLOWS EXISTING SHAPE

STEP 1

Draw any open shape. I've started with a soft, rounded heart to give me an interesting line to follow.

STEP 2

Your next line should follow along the shape you drew in Step 1.

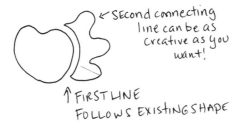

STEP 3

Now, where there is no existing shape (empty space), you may draw any line you choose in order to close the shape. For instance, here I've drawn a line that followed the shape in a smooth fashion, but then I've reconnected the lines with a wavy line (not like the smooth rounded first line I drew in Step 2).

STEP 4

Repeat this example, following the existing line of your previous shape to make your first line, and then close your new shape in a creative way.

Drawing
in between
shapes

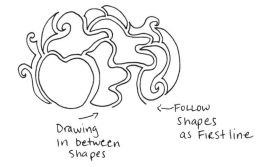

Drawing
in between
shapes

←—FOLLOW
shapes
as First line

STEP 5

If you draw between shapes, then you should
follow those shapes, just like a puzzle piece
would have to fit the shapes around it to snap
into place.

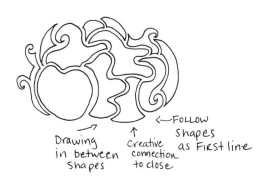

Drawing
in between
shapes

↑
Creative
connection
to close

←—FOLLOW
shapes
as First line

ART POINT

*When we learn something new, our brains try to see if it
matches something we already know so it can categorize it
quickly, like already having a road paved to get there. This
can be helpful when recalling similar tasks help you learn
the new thing. However, in some cases, the brain has to
build a new highway for different information. It is okay
if something is a little challenging, because you might be
creating new information highways inside your brain.*

Break It Down

**How would you draw that object? Begin with the most basic
discernable shape. Start with what you know.**

When inspired by a pattern, try to identify the most basic shape
so you can draw it easily. Complicated designs often begin with a small
shape—a circle, triangle, square, or maybe just a straight line. They only look
complicated because a series of other consistent (or inconsistent) patterns
have joined the party.

Once you are good at breaking down patterns to their core, you will discover that
skill to be a tool you can use in life. When people are emotional, or get triggered by
something, a person who is keen at finding patterns will be more capable of picking
up on what the basic starting point was for the emotional person's behavior or actions.
For instance, it is pretty easy to tell when a person has just gotten off the phone with
someone with whom they're in a new firecracker relationship; their eyes sparkle, they
smile easily, and they are friendly and usually more helpful. When a person is upset
after speaking with someone with whom they're in a toxic relationship, their behavior
and actions will not reflect those of a person with a new lover. People's actions and
behaviors are a reaction to the connections they have with others, and their emotional responses might not have anything to do with you.

Not only can learning to spot, interpret, and create patterns help you to
understand others better, but it can help you establish better coping
mechanisms and perhaps help you identify your own core issues by
making you capable of seeing the basic shape of your emotional responses. Recognizing what brings pleasure or
frustration to human beings is definitely a result of
understanding patterns.

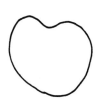

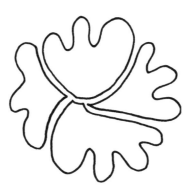

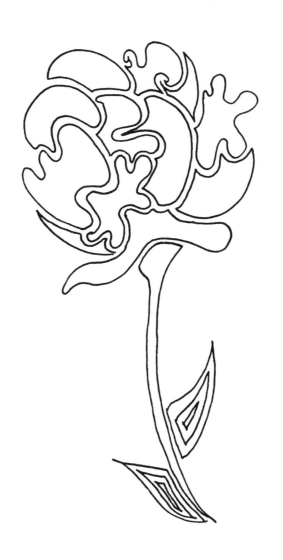

Drawing Lines for Movement

Lines all by themselves can be really neat designs and you will easily find inspiration for line work in items like wood grain, veins in leaves, and flower petals, as well as in the structures of butterfly and dragonfly wings. Drawing lines in a row, with or without a particular plan, can give a fascinating perspective on the movement of lines, which is harder to see in just one line. See how these lines build upon themselves and have different outcomes.

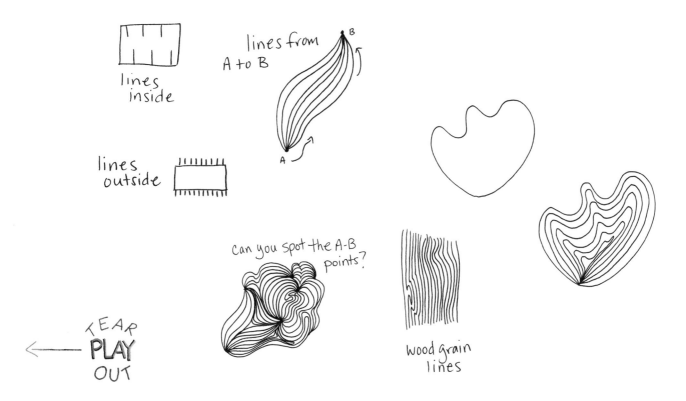

lines inside

lines from A to B

lines outside

Can you spot the A-B points?

TEAR
PLAY
OUT

wood grain lines

STEP 1

Here is a project using line movement within shapes, First, I've created free form shapes, spaced out from each other on the paper. (You can create any free forms you like.)

STEP 2

Here I've drawn concentric lines, inside each open shape made in Step 1. This creates a dramatic change with simple lines following the shape's basic design. Putting lines close together will have a different look than spacing them far apart.

MANDALAS AND MORE

STEP 3

For added effect, I used black ink in all the white areas surrounding each puzzle piece shape to make the shapes really stand out!

STEP 4

To create dimension, here I used small dots on the edges of each shape for a shadow effect.

Lollipops to Bloom

This project works with recognizable shapes and incorporates transitions! Watch for gradual changes as well as how a single change can make a dynamic shift in the formation of this image. This project demonstrates how you can move between different shapes while building.

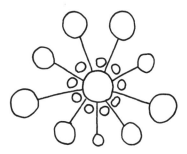

STEP 1

Start with a circle in the middle. This is your seed. I've placed small circles around the edge to create something interesting.

STEP 2

Draw a series of lollipop designs around the edge. They can be straight or wiggly. I've drawn mine as straight lines—think lollipop sticks here. Rotate your page to make drawing your lines easy and effortless as you go around your shape.

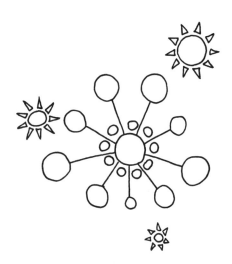

STEP 3

Next draw a few more shapes randomly around your existing shape. I've drawn three small circles, the same as I did in Step 1, but in different sizes, with triangles instead of small circles around the edges. Turn your page as necessary when drawing the triangles.

STEP 4

Trace an outline around your shapes. Notice how I've traced an outline around the center lollipop design, following exactly the same shape as the lollipops. (Remember to rotate your page as you draw an outline.) Two of the additional circles with the triangles have pointed outlines, while the upper right circle with triangles has a soft, rounded outline. By simply adding an outline, I have instantly expanded my drawing. You can choose what your outline looks like in order to expand your drawing in whatever way you think best.

MANDALAS AND MORE

STEP 5

I liked the ease of building the first pattern, so I've drawn a series of lollipops on the three outer shapes. Look carefully at the subtle differences of adding lollipops. Notice on the shape to the left, I've added lollipops on both the points and the deep divots. To the shape on the bottom, I've added small circles on the tippy top of the points and then lollipops on the deep divots, to accommodate for its small size. Then I've outlined all three outer flowers—which I now call flowers because that's how I've begun to really see them.

STEP 6

This is where the real fun begins. If you wish, you can embrace the color of your pen in all these exercises, but in this case black really helps to create shape and add definition to the small circles in each of the lollipops. Make small designs, working with one flower at a time all the way around before moving onto the next flower. Add a pattern of your choice to the exact center circle of each flower as well. Benoit Mandelbrot reminds us, "The beauty of geometry is that it is a language of extraordinary subtlety that serves many purposes."

STEP 7

Add some leaf shapes around your entire image, starting by creating leaves closest to the flowers. I've chosen pointed petals for this picture, but you can make yours round. If you feel like your leaf pattern is a little bare, you can do as I did and add a few leaves with a second layer between each leaf to make it expand a little farther. Overall, your image does not have be perfectly symmetrical or absolutely round.

STEP 8

Inside the center area is a large open white space. Filling it in with a simple texture background will make it interesting and help your center flower pop forward in design. This is a pattern I make by putting small lines from all four directions, horizontal, vertical, diagonal left, and diagonal right. I draw three lines in one of the directions, counting in my head "one, two, three," and then I switch directions and draw another set of three lines. This is an easy way to add texture and fill in a space. You can study the texture in the full scale example at the end of the project.

STEP 9

Continue filling with texture in any background that falls behind the other flowers. Next, draw a slightly wavy line down the center of each leaf, as I've done here. You could draw a straight line down the center, but a slightly wavy line can give the leaf the appearance of movement—even to you—as you build your next pattern.

STEP 10

Pick one side of your leaf to make a pattern. I've chosen to draw two stripes on the left side of each leaf. Notice that I've left the right sides open.

Any open space can hold a pattern, be colored in, or be left open to add interest to an overall design. Relax and be flexible in using this technique to change the impact a small space can have on a larger design.

STEP 11

Color in the stripes from Step 10, all the way around. Look at the design with the colored stripes in place first before deciding to add any additional details to that side. If you want, add a single line and a small dot at the end between each of the middle stripes on the left side of each petal. Do this all the way around before adding any additional patterns.

Less is more in pattern building. Doing a single pattern all the way around allows you to see what that pattern does all by itself. People who try to do too much too soon will find themselves frustrated when they can't remember what pattern they did first or how they got there. Let one pattern show you what it looks like first before you decide on a second one. Who knows? You might come up with an idea based solely on seeing the pattern all the way around.

STEP 12

Decide on a pattern for the right side of the leaf. I've drawn small circles from the bottom to about halfway up the right side of each leaf drawing, putting the largest circle at the bottom and making them smaller and smaller as I've gone up.

STEP 13

Outline the leaves all the way around by drawing a new line just outside the entire design's edge. Add a small texture pattern inside this new space between the outer line and the leaf line. I've drawn simple straight lines all the way around to frame my entire image and make my leaves stand out. You can chose any small pattern or even color the whole thing in to create a frame around your leaves.

TEAR
PLAY ⟶
OUT

Chapter Three

Building Patterns with a Prompt

"What you do today can improve all your tomorrows."
—RALPH MARSTON

Foundations are the base line to build upon that sustains any structure. A solid foundation can create support for your home or for your health. Foundations can also give you a jumping-off place on which to be challenged and creative, because the ground is established, ready for you to build upward and outward! A flat surface is a much easier foundation on which to build a house of cards, especially for the beginner who has to learn patience and awareness in handling the thin paper cards.

By now, you have practiced the fundamentals of holding your pen in a relaxed way, learned how to create patterns by putting simple lines together. You probably started to notice designs all around you with more observant eyes, as well. You might have already begun to add them to your practice pages or maybe to the pattern library's open pages in the back of the book. You have also created freehanded pattern building designs from easy to intricate. With all this—plus the ideas of Adjust, Breathe, and Connect—you create a stronger internal foundation of awareness. Do this simple practice today, and you build a calm, curious, connected, and intrigued version of what life has to offer you tomorrow. Not to mention constant improvement of your amazing drawing skills!

Are you ready to try foundation drawing from a form–shape base? It is definitely different than freeform development. This chapter can provide a whole new world of play for those who enjoy taking "something" and turning it into "something else." In classes, when these concepts are brought in, students often enjoy incorporating their freedom of development to these pattern-building challenges.

Sometimes, when students are unsure of where to begin a design or they want to create from a different starter position, they will begin a drawing from the following examples. I will introduce you to templates, such as cookie cutters, squiggly lines, and word play with letters. Enjoy!

Templates

Templates are patterns "used to guide the form of a piece being made," according to the Merriam-Webster dictionary. Let your imagination feel relaxed and creative. The easiest template you can make is to simply draw a shape to create from. Try something simple like a circle, triangle, square, or spiral and begin to build patterns on, in, or around the shape. Any basic shape can provide a template to build from. Your first shape does not have to be complicated. As a matter of fact, the simpler the better, so you can build off of it easily. If you begin to load your paper too quickly with too many shapes, you will likely learn that all those extra shapes will limit pattern building ideas because all the space is already taken. Here are some examples of easy starter shapes.

Trace a shape.

I originally introduced this idea in classes as a means to use something familiar and build something creative from it. The traced shape acts as a frame. It is in essence a template, but is a little more creative in that you are working with an existing shape. Like with the frame of a house, you can build inside and outside of this framework. My favorite is to trace cookie cutters that have interesting shapes.

Cookie cutter shapes I have enjoyed using as templates are: a bell, a heart, a foot, and a butterfly.

Sometimes you might wonder how to start a drawing. Templates can come from shapes you trace: a small square tissue box, the base of a drinking glass, or a business card. Use the handle of a kitchen spoon or a shot glass for a small circle, or a quarter for a smaller circle.

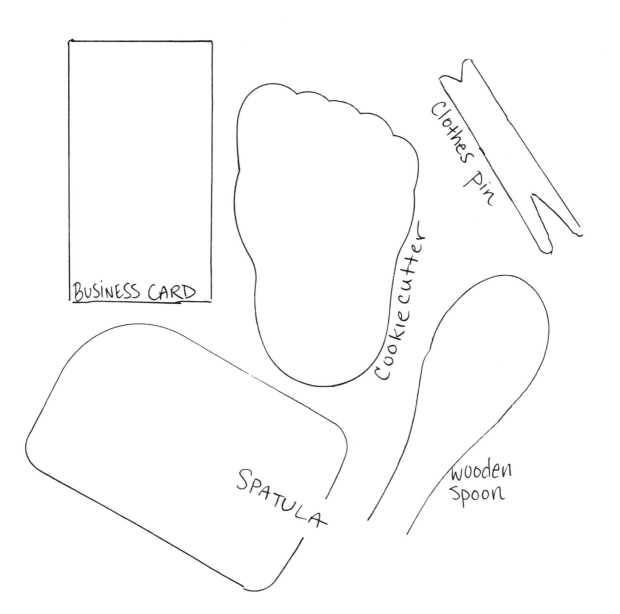

BUSINESS CARD

Clothes Pin

Cookie cutter

SPATULA

Wooden Spoon

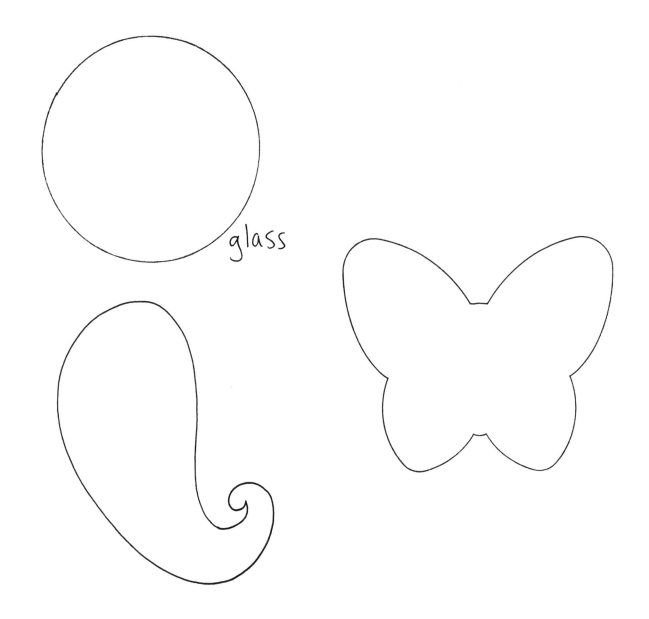

glass

Nesting Hearts

Let's practice with a group of nesting cookie cutters that make concentric hearts as templates to play with patterns. This time I'm going to show you the exact steps I'm taking before they are done so you can see them as small units, like ingredients in a recipe.

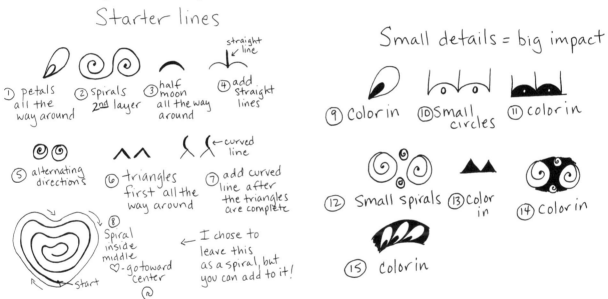

PATTERN LINES

Each pattern above is listed numerically in the order in which it was drawn. Pattern line number 1 was drawn all the way around the heart before drawing the lines from pattern number 2.

EMBELLISHMENT DETAILS

None of the details were planned in advance; they were simply created after seeing the impact of the previous lines and details.

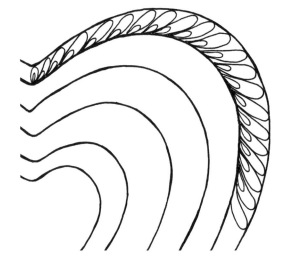

STEP 1

First I traced a series of heart-shaped cookie cutters. Then, with each step, I did a single pattern all the way around to let it show itself to me. I began with a double-layer petal on the outside heart layer. I made sure my pen moved to touch the inside edge, then all the way out to the outside edge, and back again to the inside edge.

NOTE: I am going to show you close ups so you can use them as a guide to the development.

STEP 2

Using a swirly "S" shape, I slowly and carefully filled in the second layer of the heart.

STEP 3

You'll begin to notice I created a different but simple pattern for each layer. This layer was an easy half-moon shape placed close enough to each other so they just touch.

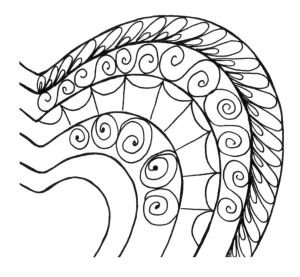

STEP 4

Add straight lines from the base of each half-moon shape. This one line will change the whole layer's overall appearance.

STEP 5

In the next layer, add spiral circles in alternating directions, clockwise and counter-clockwise.

STEP 6

Add small triangles to the next layer. Give them a bit of space between each one so they are not touching one another. Hint: If you draw each straight line individually, it will prevent a lazy triangle from showing up. Consistency helps as the patterns develop.

STEP 7

Add a slight "C" shaped line from the top of the triangle to the edge of the layer. The small curve, instead of a straight line, unexpectedly gives the illusion of overlapping hearts in this layer.

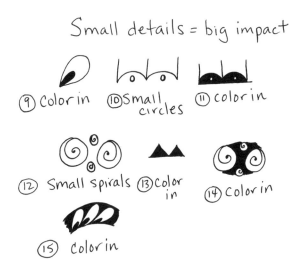

Small details = big impact

⑨ Color in ⑩ Small circles ⑪ color in

⑫ Small spirals ⑬ Color in ⑭ Color in

⑮ Color in

STEP 8

The very center heart is unique in that it is not a layer but rather a full shape. Starting from the bottom, trace an inner outline, spiraling inward, keeping the spacing the same as you move inward toward the center. This will make it easier for you to build off of later, if you choose.

EMBELLISHMENT DETAILS

Next is where the small inky details begin to make further shifts in the appearance of the drawing.

STEP 9

Ink in only the small center of the petal pattern from your first layer. Do this all the way around.

STEPS 10 & 11

Draw small circles in the half-moon shapes from the third layer. Keep your circles open (not dots) so you can ink around them for layer 11. This way they can look like little lights shining through.

STEP 12

Add small spirals in the spaces between your larger spiral circles from layer five.

STEP 13

Ink in the triangles you drew in layer six. Move mindfully so your triangle edges maintain their straight edges. Take your time; enjoy the process.

STEP 14

Carefully ink in the areas around the spiral circles in layer five. You'll begin to see the line between layer five and six disappear.

STEP 15

To bring out the edge of your heart and give it a stronger presence, go back to layer number one and ink in the area around the outside of your larger petal.

THE BIG PICTURE

Learn to Admire and Appreciate

For an artist to step back and really admire any work they do is so satisfying, whether it is drawing with ink or coloring a design they created, or even coloring in a coloring book like *The Artful Mandala Coloring Book* or *The Ancient Alchemy Coloring Book*. In classes, workshops, and presentations, I am always on the lookout for that gratifying sound mixed with surprise when someone actually "sees" their work. Did you know that smiles are more powerful than chocolate, sex, or money on the pleasure-inducing centers of the brain? British researchers discovered that the response to genuine smiles naturally elevates our happiness!

I encourage all artists in every stage of development to take pictures of their work while it is in different stages. For the beginner it is so incredibly helpful to learn how to look at an image in its entirety, without their eagle eye on what they see as a single, flawed line. Taking a picture, which is so easy to do with smartphones, mobile devices, and cameras with digital screens, can give you a chance to step away from your close view of the details and see with a larger vision your full piece of art. This is how I encourage you to see value in your work, as if it were a professional commission for a gallery—with admiration, respect for your art, and pride in knowing, "I did that!"

Small admirations of your own work build confidence and increase the chances of your admiration for another's art as well. When you, as an artist—you, yes, you—feel a flutter of awe in your heart, you know you have created a natural rhythm with your pen and the paper, and this is the beginning of real self-respect. Remember Lao Tzu's sage advice? "A journey of a thousand miles begins beneath one's feet."

TEAR
PLAY
OUT

Squiggle Line

If you're ready to go beyond straight lines and traditional shapes, squiggles are an unexpected and fun way to begin patterns. Consider that this tactic is like a skeleton with which to build patterns upon. Add your inspired patterns based on what the squiggle shares with you design-wise. These patterns can have a completely open starting place with an untamed line drawn across the page. These will feel different than a structured template or a traced shape. Squiggle drawings can look familiar, or, if choosing more fluid or bold edges, they can be abstract or imaginative representations. Squiggles have no rules. This exercise is perfect for the person seeking something new and different with which to begin a drawing.

STEP 1

Draw any squiggly, non-linear line you like. I chose a wavy zigzag that ended with a loose spiral. I have no plans or preconceived ideas of what this will ultimately look like.

STEP 2

As I began to choose patterns, I added small leaf loops along the entirety of the squiggle line. Next, I added a half-moon, petals of varying shapes, and I even included a few extra squiggle line vines. Remember: There are no rules with squiggles!

STEP 3

Continue this process along the squiggle. See if you can start to make the original line disappear. One way to make this happen is to add patterns away from the squiggle so your eyes have more areas of interest to explore.

STEP 4

Add repeating patterns in areas that are open and available. Making use of dots and divots is a wonderful way to add whimsy and continue the organic theme in a squiggle drawing.

TEAR
PLAY ⟶
OUT

Name Frame

Name Frame is a playful technique using letters. There are three ways to play with letters, and I have projects for each of these that draw on the work you've already done. In the direct approach, the letters are open templates that you can draw in and around.

The wire frame approach uses multiple lines to evoke movement. The hidden name frame is a game my students love. In this method, you start with letters and then build patterns in and around them until the word becomes invisible.

Direct Name Frame

In the direct approach, use the letters like a template and fill in the spaces with any designs you like. You've probably seen this approach used in birthday cards (now you can make your own), signage, home décor, and business marketing. By noticing your patterns in ink or colored in, you can get different ideas on designs.

STEP 1

Draw any name or initials you want to play with for a pattern template. For this example, I used ABC.

STEP 2

Mindfully design each letter carefully, using a variety of patterns. You can even get playfully "out of the box" like I did with the letter "B" and allow your design to move in an unexpected way beyond the letter's defining edge.

Wire Frame Name Frame

Wire Frames can literally be used in any multimedia art form, from garden sculptures to ornaments to more elaborate structures such as base skeletons—to be used for an animated puppet or even an articulated stuffed animal that bends at the knees and elbows. Wire Frames are also used as the most primary lines, to create the structure of a physical body such as a stick figure. For our purposes, we will be using a Wire Frame of a word—name, special place, symbolic meaning, it's up to you!—to give direction on line movement. You'll still be able to see the word, but it will look very different from the direct technique you completed.

STEP 1

Write down in clean lines any name or word that comes to mind. I used the word "love."

STEP 2

Use the technique shown in the project Drawing Lines for Movement. You are not limited by any shape or form here, since your lines will simply connect from one letter to another letter. Experiment. Be imaginative. Can you still see your original word?

TEAR PLAY ⟶ OUT

LOVE

Hidden Name Frame

This project is by far the favorite among my students. Using a word of your choice, you can either write cleanly and clearly or you can hint at the letters, placing them at different areas rather than in a straight line. I'll show you both examples. Using the letters, build different patterns incorporating the letters with the intention of making the original word disappear in the final drawing. It's fun to experiment with a group of people using the same word and having the drawings come out completely differently.

STEP 1

Write a word clearly so you can see all the letters. Scan or take a picture of your original word, if you can. Using all your techniques, slowly build the patterns to make the word disappear.

STEP 2

It's fun to watch your art go through transformation as you hide the original word. As a helpful hint to remember what word you used, I often write the word somewhere on the edge of the finished project.

Here's an example of "hinting" the letters of the name.

STEP 1

Write the letters in a way that hints the letter without completing the lines. Change up the placement of the letters by having them dance in the space rather than be in a straight line. Take a picture or scan your original word, if possible.

STEP 2

Using any patterns that interest you, draw them and simply watch the name transform. Be inspired to move to a different pattern through observation. This is an example of an unexpected outcome. I was not even thinking of any solid forms, but the patterns I started to draw grew in such a way that I began to see branches and a bird!

MANDALAS AND MORE

Tundra

LOVE JOY

Chapter Four

Meditative Mandalas

"Let the waters settle and you will see the moon and
the stars mirrored in your own being."
—RUMI

Mandalas have a rich history spanning several cultures, and they have different names around the world. In Sanskrit, mandala translates literally to mean "circle." Mandalas originally were representative of the cosmic whole. As time moved forward and cultures borrowed from the geometric designs of their predecessors, they created a calm arrangement of repetitive patterns in layers, most often in circular fashion. There are also the Buddhist square configurations representing the four gates (the four directions), and the Hindu yantras (geometrical designs referencing specific deities).

Traditionally, color is an important aspect of mandalas, as each individual color has cultural significance, especially in Buddhism. The colors help define the importance of the layers by visually indicating each one's meaning.

The deepest representations of wholeness and happiness are almost always present in a mandala but they do not represent happiness itself. It is, after all, our job to find happiness, but mandalas can act as a directory or legend on a map of our journey. If you would like to investigate the deeper meanings of the detailed symbolism of ancient mandalas, I encourage you to look at their history through the cultures and beliefs of Buddhism, Hinduism, Jainism, and even Christianity.

In this chapter, you will be given the basics on creating nonsecular mandalas with and without a circular grid.

Grids, if formally used, fall in the category of tools. In my classes, I like to teach beginners how to draw mandalas without a grid so they can develop a sense of spacing and muscle memory through shape building, trusting that the outcome will be reflective of their drawing (or spiritual) development if they use the techniques as described: *be mindful, go slow, connect to the pen and paper, let the pattern emerge, and rotate your paper.*

But if you would like to approach mandalas with a more systematic or more precise building method, a grid will be helpful. If you have access to a light table, you can place the supplied grid beneath any drawing paper as a guide. If not, you can draw a grid directly on your paper with very light pencil markings—the only time I will suggest sketching anything before using a pen.

Point-to-Point (PTP)

You'll use the point-to-point technique in this chapter. Point-to-point, or PTP, is as simple as it sounds—drawing a line from one point to another point. The concept is quite unassuming when you first start, but focusing on how you move from one point to another point is where some interesting diversions can occur in a pattern's overall development. Be mindful of the simplicity of PTP; this is where magical and even sophisticated patterns can develop without the over-complications of focusing too hard on introducing complex details.

Drawing PTP can be done in a variety of ways, but it is ALWAYS, always, always, done simply and with *one* line at a time. If you combine multiple lines in succession you are making a pattern, and that is different than PTP.

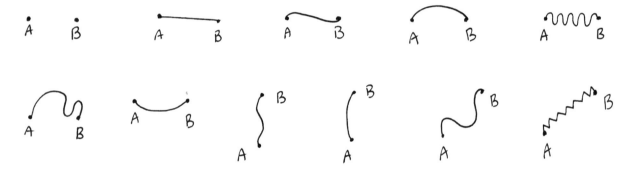

Outward In Mandala

You will learn about two different mandala creations in this section: two mandalas organically built and two mandalas based on a grid. For the first project, start with a large circle and systematically move toward the center. When creating mandalas, be mindful of your pen-and-paper contact; you'll enjoy the process and be much more satisfied with the end result if you take your time. Let's begin.

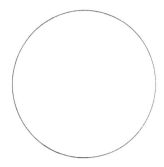

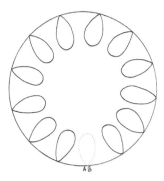

STEP 1

Apply your ABCs in a mindful body scan. Draw a basic circle shape that is almost as large as your paper. Give yourself some room to work inside this circle. You can create a circle by tracing a cup or bowl or plate. I have a favorite size plate for a certain size paper that I use when I want a quick outer starter circle for mandalas.

STEP 2

For this exercise we will begin from the outside edge just so the beginner artist can see how PTP can build from a point that is farther from the center. Draw a single PTP from a selected point A to a selected point B. Here, I've decided that my point A and my point B will be the same place—I've looped back around to start. Repeat the PTP all the way around the circle.

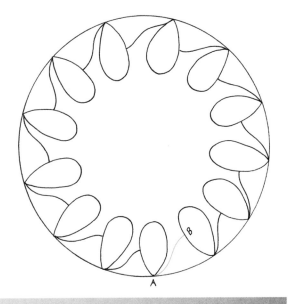

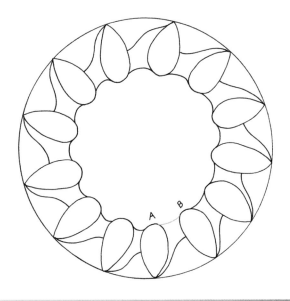

STEP 3

Pick a secondary point A to point B connection. No rushing, no deciding beforehand how you think you want this to look. Let the pattern emerge on its own by allowing it to develop with these simple line connections. Make it easy: be consistent, be patient, and draw simply. Repeat the same PTP all the way around.

STEP 4

Continue this process until you reach the center. Follow the examples set by the initial PTP and see how your drawing develops into a pattern by doing one line all the way around. Remember, no rushing the pattern!

Let the pattern show you what it can do in this design method.

You can add details
with patterns or color.

MANDALAS AND MORE

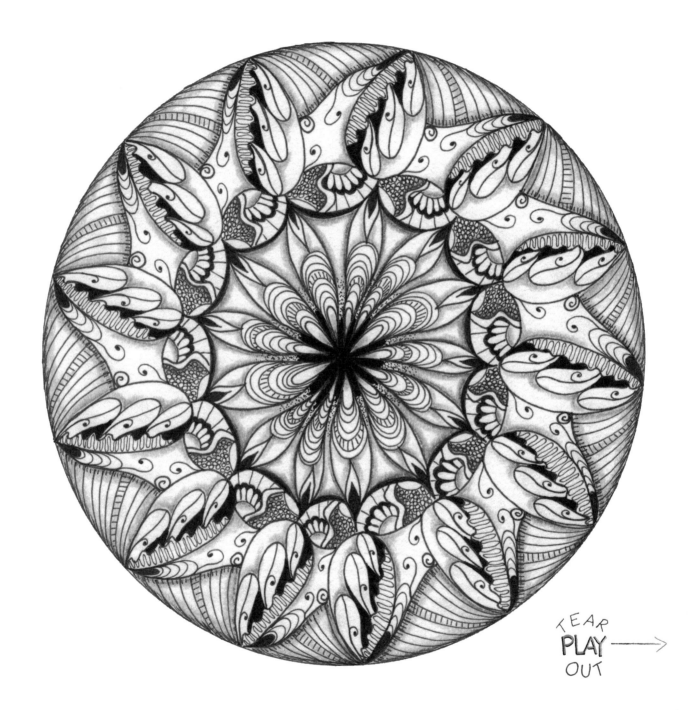

TEAR
PLAY →
OUT

Inward Out Mandala

Now let's explore using the center as a building block in developing design. In this example I will not be tracing an outer circle to start off, but instead will allow my design to create the circle through simply using the PTP method.

STEP 1

Remember the Body Scan ABCs. Create a shape to build your PTP lines off of. Here, I've placed a small circle in the center to represent the larger circular pattern I intend to build. This is still a simple point A to point B connection—both points just happen to be in the same place to make a circle.

STEP 2

Begin with a PTP from a starting point A to an ending point B. In this case, I've connected my PTP lines so they anchor to the original center circle. This helps guide my developing lines to the larger circular mandala I am creating. You can see how this technique also helps to establish a symmetry that acts somewhat as a compass, where the directions north, south, east, and west appear in the mandala. This visualization helps me point the lines in the right direction. I find it much easier to draw each PTP if I remember to rotate my paper.

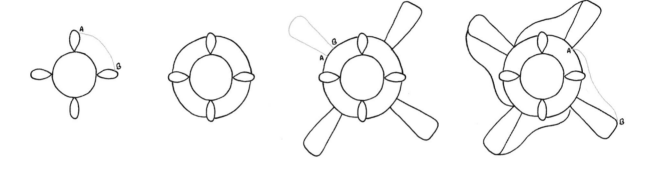

Continue this PTP pattern, always one line at a time, in easy, simple ways, to build the mandala outward in a gentle, consistent pattern. Be mindful of the ABC Body Scans and rotate your paper for easy drawing.

Keep going, adding on as you go.

MANDALAS AND MORE

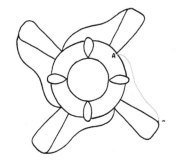

164

Embellishing Your Mandala

I kept going and embellishing my mandala, using the elements below.

See if you can find the matching pieces. (This helps stimulate pattern recognition—like pattern hide-and-seek!)

Give yourself a chance to play with PTP, building from the outer edge inward like the preceding examples. Pick a Point A and a Point B, making both points touch the circle, just to get you started. Then build from there, slowly. Remember, be mindful, go slow, connect to the pen and paper, let the pattern emerge, *and rotate your paper.*

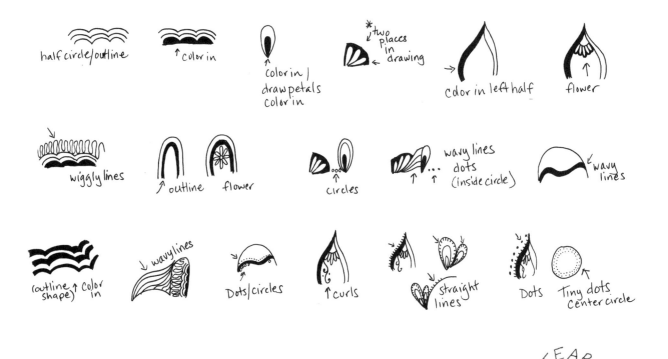

MANDALAS AND MORE

Breathe

**The best way to begin anything new is to breathe, both in and out.
Don't hold your breath!**

Breath is so important. When we hold our breath, unconsciously we stop the flow of life. In Jin Shin Jyutsu, the art of harmonizing energy in the body, it is taught that we never "take" a breath. Taking implies grabbing something with nothing in return. In actuality, there is a constant exchange of oxygen and carbon dioxide. Oxygen is needed for cellular respiration, feeding the cells new life as it changes to a usable identity in the bloodstream. The body then releases the byproduct of this process in the form of carbon dioxide. This byproduct is the exact form of "oxygen" plants require, creating a symbiotic relationship between us and other living entities.

When we remember to breathe, or relearn to breathe, in a relaxed, free-flowing way, our relationship with the exchange of life around us softens. Art is often a reflection of or a translation of emotions. Some emotions are similar to the feeling of holding our breath. We can allow breath to guide our state of being to further connectivity and approach drawing from a calm place within our bodies and minds.

Circular Grids

Making a mandala by using a circular grid is easier in some ways because you can see your spacing exactly, so there is no guessing if you are off a little or a lot in the overall design. To me the energy is a little different because the grid itself holds a stability in its presence and can act as either a crutch or a support, depending on what the artist's attitude is with regard to development. In classes, I do not use grids because I would rather the artist develop muscle memory that allows them to create with a consistency of line, space, and scale, eventually trusting the overall process of organic pattern development. However, I do think every artist should learn how to use grids and see if they are something they like to work with, or at least to see what effect a grid has on their process.

Grid work can allow the artist to achieve precise detail and create a wonderful overall effect in mandala design.

Included here is a circular grid that can be used for practicing on your own paper. There are several pages included in this book for you to practice line development on while using this grid, while working with the PTP method as well as any of the other pattern building styles discussed so far. If you have access to a light table or light board, where the surface illuminates your papers so you can see through the them (a clean window will work, too!), this will give you more ease in seeing the grid lines when you place the grid underneath a separate sheet of paper. The light will also help you to draw more cleanly.

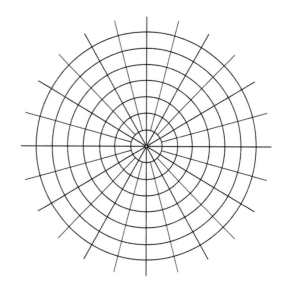

ART POINT

You can create your own circular grid by using a ruler and measuring halfway down the page in both directions, creating light lines at 90 degrees in the center. Imagine you are cutting slices of pizza into equal triangles from here and you can draw a series of fairly evenly spaced lines. If you want completely accurate lines and spacing, I suggest using a compass or protractor.

Mandala with Grid

Some people will enjoy the presence of a structured line, so it will be easy to use the grid system. However, feel free to use the grid as a guideline, not as an absolute basis to create your lines and patterns. Get creative as you go, play with your spacing to build subtle changes that can soften hard straight lines.

STEP 1

Decide what your first PTP line will be and if it will move from the center outward or from the outer edge inward. I've started this example with a center point and am going to build outward. I drew a very small circle in the center, then used the grid lines to guide my steps. In the enlarged example at the end you'll notice some lines intentionally go above or below the grid line, not on the grid line itself.

STEP 2

Using the grid lines as a guide, I've systematically moved in PTP fashion, slowly and gently in a line-by-line building pattern. The process is the same for each line, and with each line, I rotate my paper to increase my chances of consistency in muscle memory and line stability.

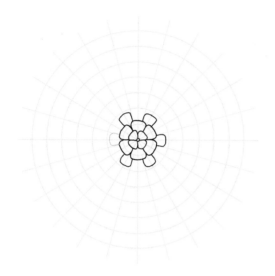

STEP 3

Continue this process as you move around the grid, building one line at a time, nothing complicated, allowing the simplicity of the lines to develop the pattern.

STEP 4

Keep going, adding on mindfully. Change the scale of your shape for added interest in design formation.

Mandalas can be created with purpose in a very specific way. I find them most enjoyable to draw when I create a rhythm with the pattern I am drawing. Finding a rhythm in the pattern will help create a calm place and consistency in your drawing.

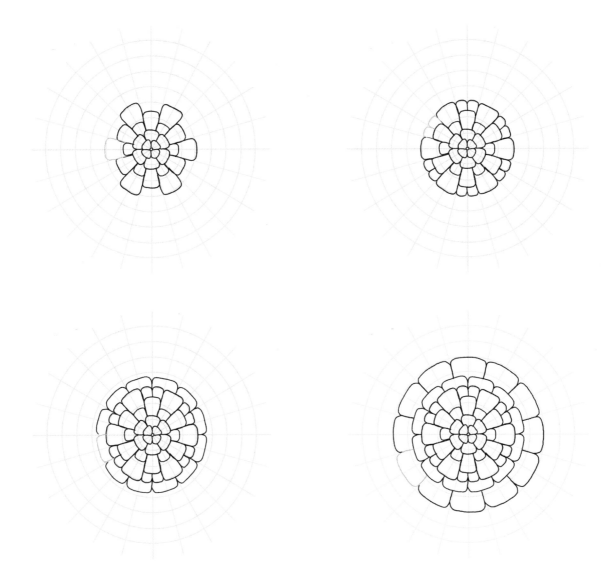

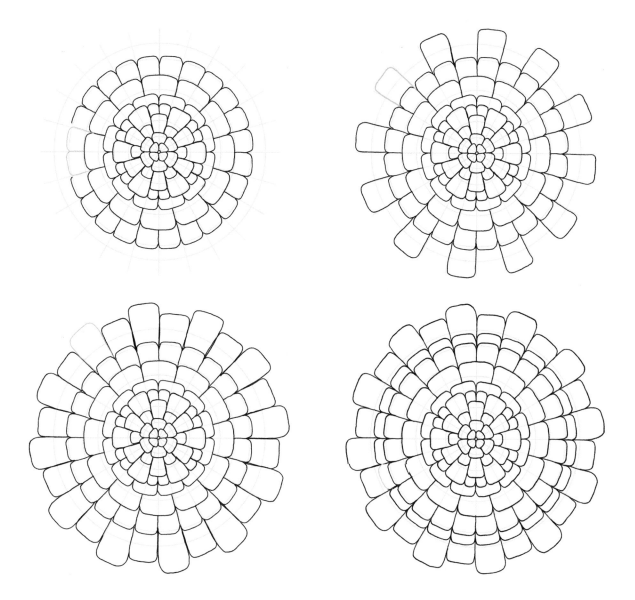

Once your mandala is complete you can add any patterns or details you want to create a very different look from your open shape mandala.

MANDALAS AND MORE

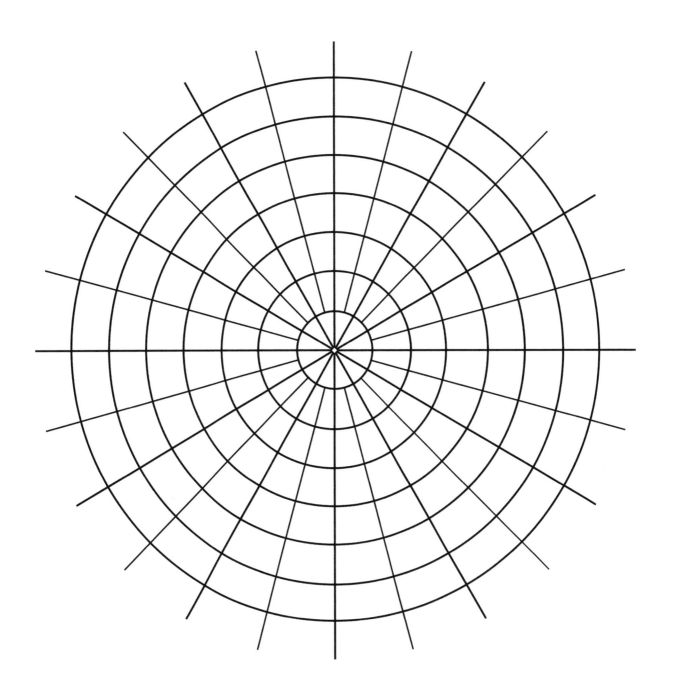

Petal Mandala with Grid

In this project, soft round curved lines will be the basic theme. You'll notice my petal loops are not between the grid lines, like one might expect, but rather use the grid line to assist in marking the center of many of the petals. This is the design used as the cover art for the book! I'll include an example of how it looked after I spent some time embellishing it with inking patterns.

STEP 1

Decide what your first PTP line will be and if it will move from the center outward or from the outer edge inward. I've started this example with a center point and am going to build outward.

STEP 2

Using the grid lines as a guide, I've systematically moved in PTP fashion, slowly and gently in a line-by-line building pattern. The process is the same for each line, and with each line, I rotate my paper to increase my chances of consistency in muscle memory and line stability.

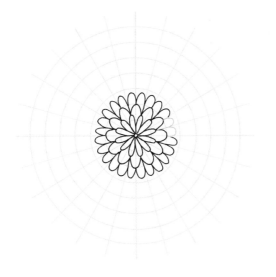

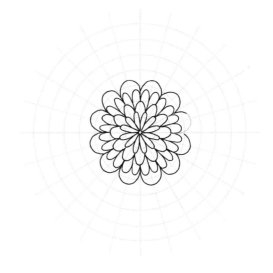

STEP 3

Continue this process as you move around the grid, building one line at a time, nothing complicated, allowing the simplicity of the lines to develop the pattern.

STEP 4

Keep going, adding on mindfully.

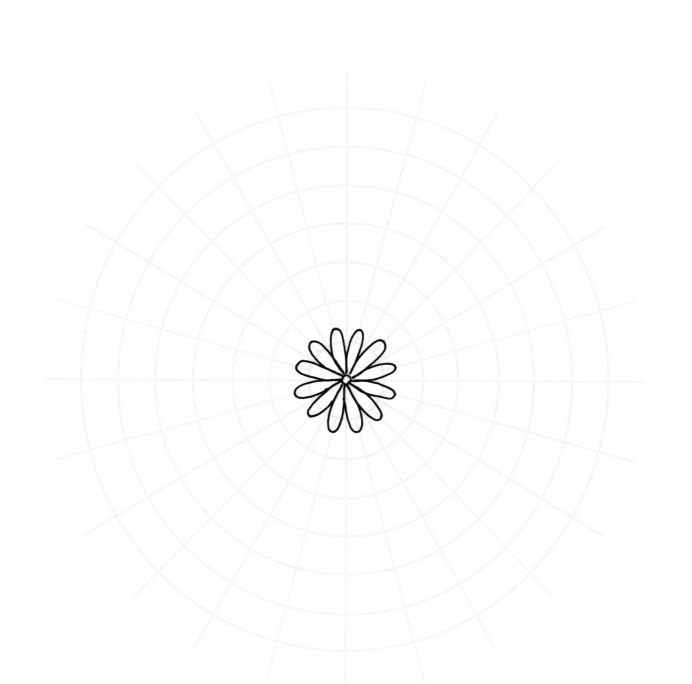

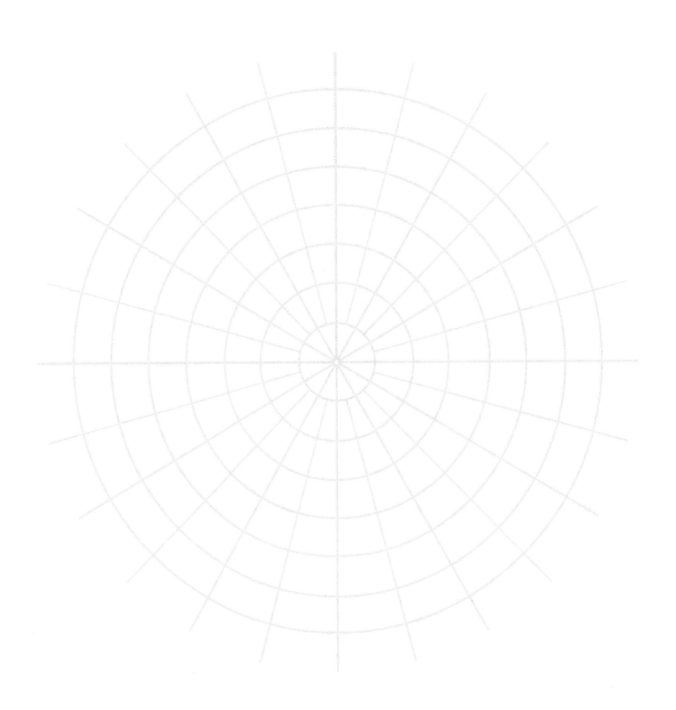

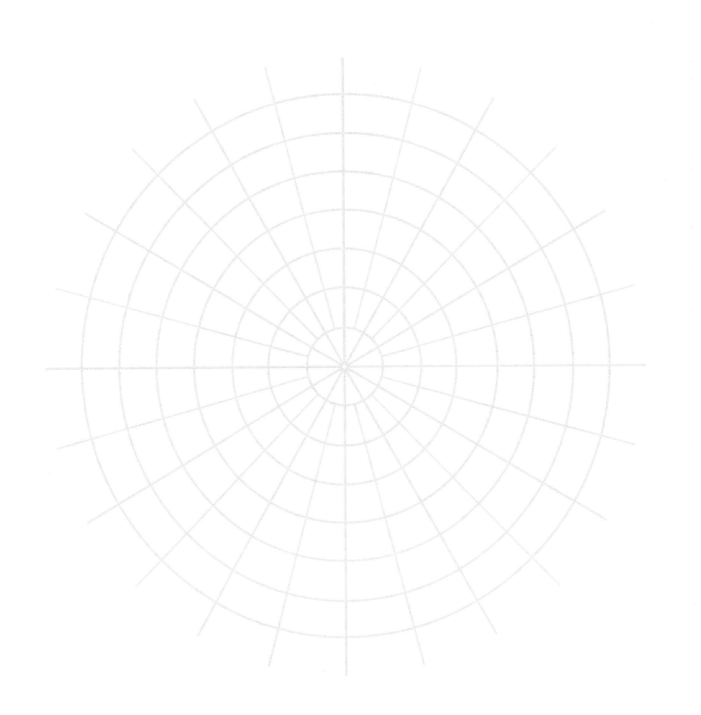

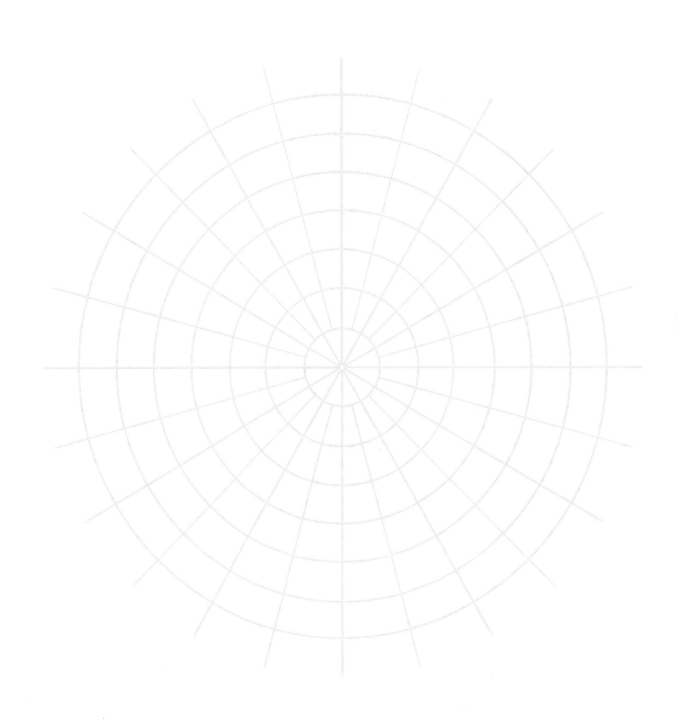

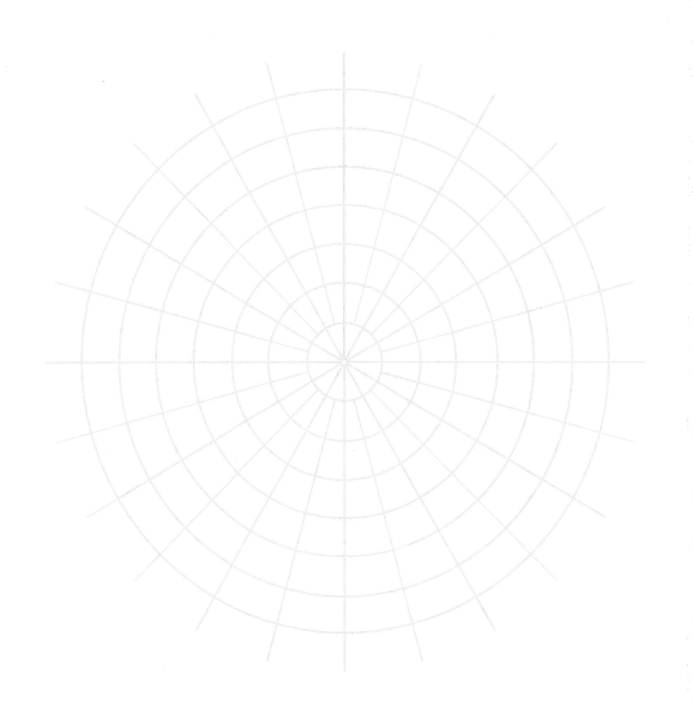

THE BIG PICTURE

Slow Down

Rushing through patterns can impact your personal vitality. Be connected to what you are doing.

In presentations, I introduce the idea of biorhythms. Similar to how the brain seeks out patterns, our body will also find a certain rhythm. Imagine the gait of horse and rider when they move together, the seamstress and sewing machine, the marching band and the music—all of these, as different as they are from each other, have rhythm in common. If the horse and rider are not in rhythm, the rider is going to be uncomfortably bouncing on top of the saddle. A seamstress who is out of rhythm with the speed of the sewing machine risks breaking a needle or bunching up the fabric. The band member who is out of rhythm with band will certainly stick out. Our bodies do similar things with internal rhythms. Our biorhythms create a repeating pattern that supports the body's natural functioning. For example, circadian rhythms are the patterns of natural sleep that the body can count on for optimal functioning.

When you slow down your drawing, you create a rhythm that mimics the gentle process of pattern building you have learned with pen and paper. The rhythm of your pen and paper makes a powerful connection to your body as it begins to join the rhythm of your focus, helping you relax with softened thoughts, tempered muscles, and open creativity. There is a Zen teaching that states, "When sleeping, just sleep. When walking, just walk. When eating, just eat." Here, we can add, "When drawing, just draw."

My experience with task-oriented people—especially women who have been trained to do more than one thing at a time—is that they have a difficult time slowing down to simply be with a single pattern. Be aware of the thinking mind's ability to catch on and move on. Let your thinking mind connect to the pattern in its entirety, and it will often relax into better communication with your creative self, allowing a rhythm to be experienced and be completely satisfying to your overall being, supporting a relaxed state I call meditative drawing.

Chapter Five

Embellishing with Shading and Color

"Life is a whim of several billion cells to be you for a while."
—GROUCHO MARX

Look at the world with new eyes and even those places and things familiar to you will become interesting. If you have learned a skill or traveled a path many times, your continued acquaintance with it creates an intimate connection that gives you a heightened level of awareness. Perhaps you have a room in which you can often tell when something looks or feels different because you are so familiar with the environment. You can become conscious of the high levels of awareness that arise from familiarity and learn to apply this consciousness to all events and observations. What's different? What's new? What's the same?

I love the depth of connection I have to the familiar way my favorite pen moves across a nice clean piece of paper. I love the way black ink creates a groundedness and a place for my eyes to rest when looking at the designs. But when I am looking for a different feeling to the overall look, I may turn to the world of graphite pencil shading or adding color. These two techniques will not only shift how a drawing looks and feels, but will deepen your ability in observing and connecting to shadows and colors around you.

In this chapter I discuss the basics in shading with graphite pencils and some basic color pencil insights. Graphite and color pencils have their own unique personalities. Remember, changing a tool means learning to work with it differently than the previous tool, ultimately expanding your knowledge and wisdom.

Pencil shading is used to create soft grays and blacks in an image that provides hints of shadow or helps to define the shape of an object. Color can be used this way as well; however, due to the nature of color, the brain is reading more than shape and shadow—it is also reading frequency or the vibration of the color. Because of this, graphite pencils can create subtle changes and softer impressions, sometimes even being overlooked because they support the existing design lines rather than a specific color. I love to use graphite to highlight an ink drawing by supporting the design.

Color can help provide a stimulus to warmth or a calming coolness to an image. If you are interested in creating art specifically to color, make sure you leave some nice open places in your design to be filled in later.

Pencil Shading

I love to approach pencil shading as something you *feel*, not something you see. It's so important to recognize the difference. This kind of shading adds dimension, character, light, and fun!

All you need is a regular pencil and a blending stick (tortillon). Actual purchased tortillons are best (see page 21). If you don't have a tortillon you can also use a Q-tip or a small, soft, clean paintbrush or a paper towel that has been twisted tightly to a create a point. For these examples, I used a number 3B pencil to make the shading a little darker for you to see.

Learning to play with shading is easy. A sharp pencil will allow you to get into tight or small spaces and let you draw in a little bit of graphite close to the area you want to shade. Make sure when drawing with pencil you *start out lighly* and work in layers if you need to go darker. The tortillon will do most of the work for you. Move the stroke of the tortillon in one of two ways: *with* the shape or in small, circular motions—not against the grain of the graphite. This action helps to "pull" the graphite away from the initial pencil line to soften the effect as it moves outward.

Playing with a pencil as a shading device can be just as meditative as it was to draw the lines of your picture. Following are some sample images to show you what a pencil can do for your drawings. Notice how they feel differently? It should feel richer and deeper in context without causing you to immediately want to say, "Oh, look at all the pencil marks." I want the viewer to still be enchanted with the design. Shading can create shadow in ways that give the impression of layers.

This technique is fun to use with any designs you draw, but it can be especially nice for adding richness to your mandalas. In the meantime, practice playing with some shading on the open practice shapes.

pencil | with bl nder (with shape) "pull" the graphite | with blender (in circles) "pull the graf...

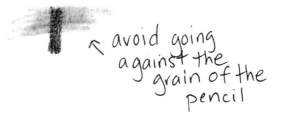

↖ avoid going against the grain of the pencil

↑EAR
PLAY ──→
OUT

Draw a line of graphite in the area you want to appear as the darkest area. Using the tortillon, gently "pull" the graphite away from the line in small circles or along the same shape as the shadow. If you lighten your pressure, the marks will also lighten.

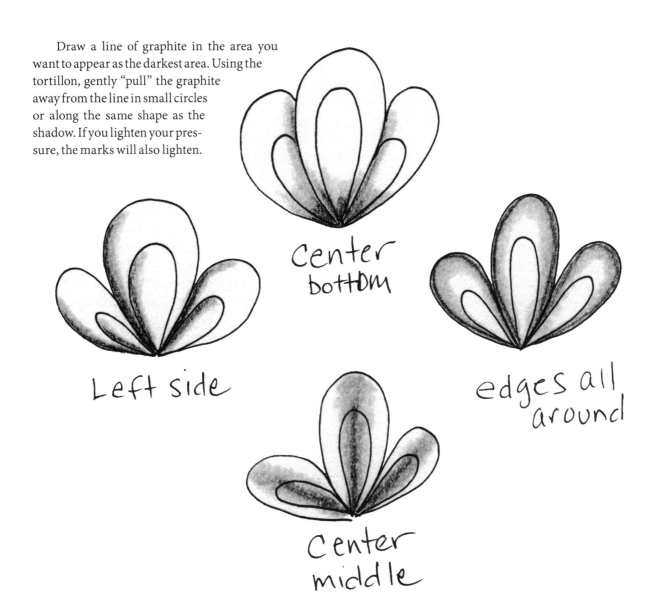

center bottom

Left side

edges all around

center middle

Hint: When a tortillon has graphite at the tip, it is now "loaded" with graphite. This happens naturally as the graphite transfers to the paper of the tortillon. You can use a "fully loaded" tortillon to add light wispy shadows to an area without having to apply the graphite directly.

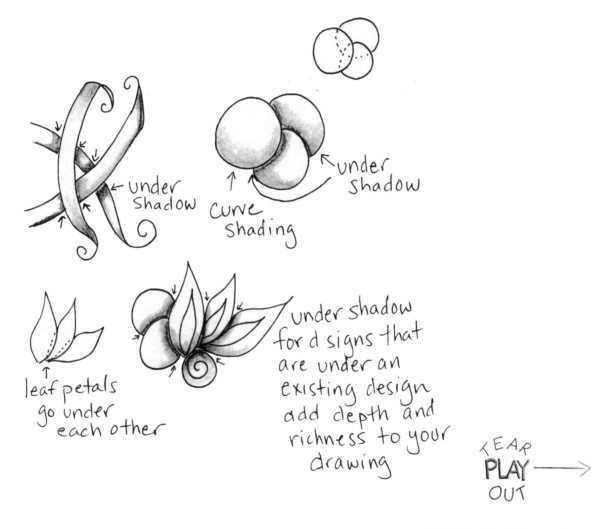

under shadow

under shadow

curve shading

leaf petals go under each other

under shadow for d signs that are under an existing design add depth and richness to your drawing

TEAR
PLAY ⟶
OUT

THE BIG PICTURE

Explore, Research, Play, and Expand

Approaching drawing with curiosity can open you to new places, new people, and new ways of seeing everything! I have had students share ideas I had not thought to use. Their excitement to explore a new way or a new tool expanded their worlds and mine! Variety is key to tapping fun and exciting creative expressions, so be willing to expand your artistic tools (pens, paper, styles, etcetera) and you may find your ability to capture a bit of whimsy from your daily life increasing. Your attitude toward realizing and enjoying the pleasures in life can mirror the fun and exploration that started with drawing.

Colored Pencil—Best Practices

I'm including a little bonus section here for those who love to color with pencils. There are some best practices you should employ when using colored pencils that will extend your enjoyment and increase your expertise.

Pencil brand. Yes, the brand of pencil you choose can make a big difference in the quality of color vitality. In addition, brands have different grades. Some pencils are designed to be softer and some harder, which makes a huge difference in the amount of color left on the paper. Some pencils come in sets and others can be purchased from open stock (meaning you can choose individual colors as needed). It will take a little investigation and practice to find out what you like to work with best.

Hard or soft pencils. Harder pencils do best with small areas and fine details. They do not dull as easily and allow for the greatest amount of *layering* through combining colors or coloring lightly and building colors gradually on top of each other. Because harder pencils do not lay down as much color as a softer wax pencil, they tend to move like graphite pencils, have a little lighter pigment (at least initially), and last a lot longer as they may not need to be sharpened as quickly as softer pencils.

Because soft pencils lay down more color at one time, keeping them sharp requires more attention in shorter intervals. Super soft pencils might leave color dust that needs to be carefully swept away (careful to not smear the dust or you'll add color to unintended areas). Soft pencils are favorites for colorists who like to *blend* colors together, which moves the wax of one color into the wax of another color.

The tooth of the paper. The "tooth" of the paper refers to its texture and surface. Most coloring books have a tooth that is fairly smooth. The tooth of the paper can be damaged and can create confusing issues for a beginning colorist. Sharp pencils allow the pigment to travel both along the top of the tooth's grooves and in between, coloring the paper's layers without damaging the tooth. Dull pencils only cover the top of the tooth, leaving interesting white spaces to show between the color. Dull pencils also have a tendency to damage the tooth when the person coloring presses harder to try to fill the white spaces. The best way to work for full coverage is to maintain a sharp pencil.

Using your pencil. For overall quality, maintain a sharp point by using a hand sharpener, and, while you are coloring, turn the pencil after several strokes to another edge of the point. This simple rotation of the contact point keeps the edge evenly sharp since all sides are in use. Think of a woman's lipstick—if you use it on only one side, you slant that side to a point, dulling the other edge to a flat surface, but if you rotated during use it would have a sharper point all the way around. Moving your pencil in small circular motions is the best way to create the most coverage, do the least amount of damage to the tooth of the paper, and gives yourself the greatest potential for layering smoothness.

Layering is key. Colored pencil enthusiasts will agree that starting out lighter and layering a little at a time will always give the most depth of color and smoothness to a final product over a single, hard pressing that flattens out the tooth. Over time, if the tooth is damaged by hard pressing, it will not allow any more pigment to adhere to the paper, which will result in a wax bloom. Wax bloom occurs when the wax begins to build and change appearance to a shine, which is a sign that the paper cannot take any more layers of color.

Blending and burnishing. Colored pencil, like any art medium, has some interesting tricks that you can investigate if you choose to move beyond simple color-on-paper techniques. The first is a variety of blending methods. Blending can be done by moving the color of one pencil into the other with a blending stump or a special blending pencil made to match an accompanying brand of colored pencil. Blending pencils are made

of the same materials and binders as colored pencils but without the pigment. Blending can take place through using just a blending pencil (dry method) or by using a blending pencil with a wet solvent such as a "blender marker" designed specifically for colored pencils. There are a variety of blending methods you can research if you are interested in experimenting.

Burnishing is a method of combining two or more surfaces to create a smoother and more cohesive finish. Color from a colored pencil can be burnished by using another pencil, such as a white pencil. Going over your color with a white pencil will lighten your layers a bit, but it will help to blend them more thoroughly. Burnishing can also be achieved with a burnishing tool, which can look like a blending pencil, but is made with a slightly harder material to help achieve a more cohesive meld of color. Burnishing with a tool can create a nice, rich shine. If you have a design that has eyes or lips or highlights (like the shine of a piece of fruit or water droplets), burnishing is a wonderful way of gaining luster. Burnishing differs from blending in that burnishing will be the final step in layering since it flattens out the tooth of the paper.

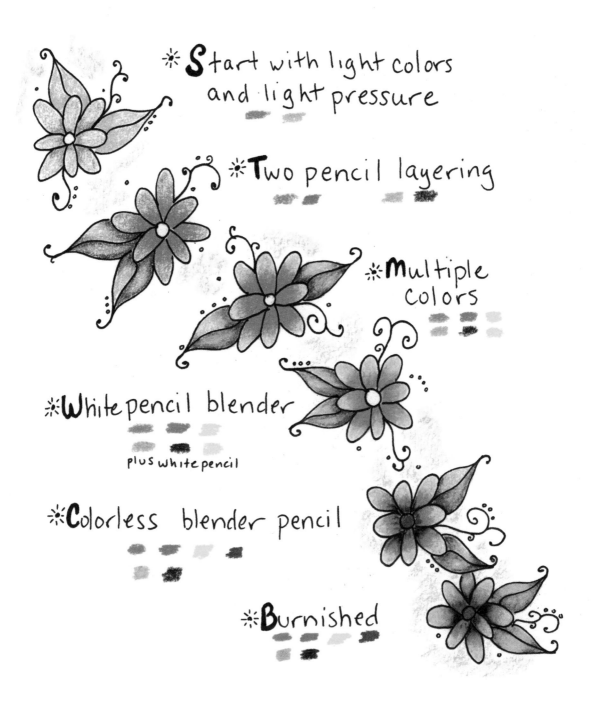

✳ **S**tart with light colors
and light pressure

✳ **T**wo pencil layering

✳ **M**ultiple colors

✳ **W**hite pencil blender

plus white pencil

✳ **C**olorless blender pencil

✳ **B**urnished

Adding a little color can be fun, creative, and relaxing.

Watch how adding more color can change the appearance of an image.

MANDALAS AND MORE

THE BIG PICTURE

Try New Tools

Have fun using pencils, pens, markers, gel pens, glitter pens, different colored tool combinations, different textures of paper, scrap paper, journals, cards, recyclable items, and more. You don't have to wait to have that special pen or paper to get started. You have all you need with a writing utensil, an appropriate surface, and your willingness to let it flow.

Sometimes, people wait for that special tool before they practice a skill, believing that it is the tool that makes the art or skill. A good storyteller only requires a story to turn it into magic. Sure, lighting or clothing or props can change how the story is perceived, but a true master needs very little to have amazing results. Use what you have and go for it!

With this in mind, trying new things to see what creative aspects you discover can be a lot of fun. When you are ready to expand your tools, you can build details or foundations with big results by making a small change to what paper you are drawing on or what pen you decide to use.

Contrast and Color for Fun

White gel pens

Use these on black paper to play with contrast. Be mindful, however, when working with white pen on black backgrounds; using the white pen strategically will have a more pleasing appearance. Overloading the paper with white ink can lose the delicate designs created.

Use white gel pens to add small highlights on top of your colored pencils, too!

White pencil

White pencil layered on top of white gel will make the lines "glow" against the black paper.

Silver and gold gel pens

Metallic gel pens can add embellishments to both your drawings and also an unexpected glimmer to an area.

Bell

This is more of a project to show you how different drawings can be completed. I will show you how the bell was created in steps for those who are curious about the process, but what I really want to show you are the last steps. I'll experiment with black ink (page 225), graphite shading (page 226), and color (page 227) to show you how different the end results can be and the possibilities you can take for each technique.

STEP 1

This bell is one of my cookie cutter templates I traced to get started. I began the inner design using the open barb feather design.

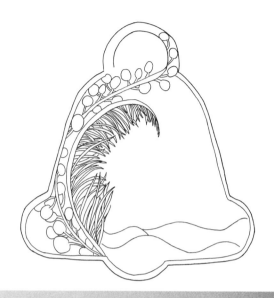

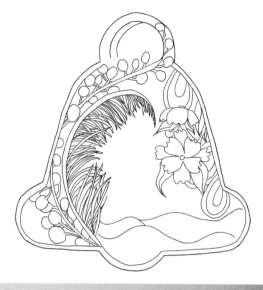

STEP 2

Next I created an open vine and added open
lollipops to create an organic feel. The wavy lines
were drawn in at the bottom and I began to see
the drawing now with more of a beach-like feel.

STEP 3

On the right hand side I drew a series of flowers
and then leaves.

STEP 4

Add whimsical dots to swirly vine-like tendrils, the flora, and the beach to create a sandy feel. Next I drew a few squiggles for a possible water area.

STEP 5

Filling in with simple line patterns in the leaves, their presence begins to change as does the details to the flower petals. In the following drawings, notice how the black ink makes an impact on the overall image.

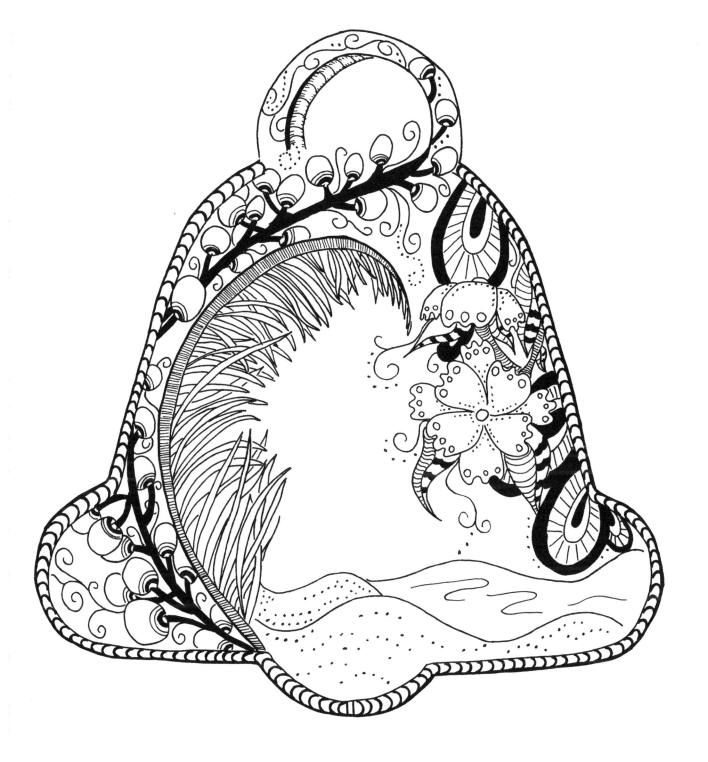

Notice What You Notice

The mere act of noticing can open a world of observation in a whole new way. (Think of hubcaps and tires on vehicles—they are all circles with different designs.)

When we create a habit of observing the world around us, we become increasingly well connected to our atmosphere, to our environment, and to our everyday places and things. The first step to being present in finding patterns in everyday life is to take a moment to observe objects, clothing, and patterns on the floor or in a picture—whatever is near you that catches your eye.

The better "seers" we are, the better we are able to discern patterns overall. When you are noticing—and this does not mean having to take action on everything you see—just notice what you notice, and sometimes you can literally watch something change before your eyes in ways you would have otherwise overlooked. In drawing, and in life, this can inspire movement and appreciation in surprising ways just because you really *saw* something, and in that seeing comes experience. This experience deepens connectivity and allows you to approach drawing from a calm place within your body and mind.

Inspirational Pattern List

Looking for inspiration can be as easy as noticing all the different patterns around you on a daily basis. Sometimes patterns hide in unexpected places. Here is a quick guide with ideas on where to look for patterns to inspire your art.

- Animals (any creatures on land, in air, and in water)
- Beading patterns
- Bedsheets, towels, pillows
- Ceilings
- Clothing (e.g., bandanas)
- Constellations
- Cultural patterns (broadly speaking, each culture has unique patterns)
- Fabric textures
- Fantasy or space pictures
- Feathers
- Flowers, plants, vines, trees, grass, reeds, bamboo, leaves
- Frames
- Gardens
- Gates
- Holiday patterns
- Hubcaps
- Ironwork
- Jewelry, chains, earrings, pendants
- Lamps, chandeliers
- Mandalas
- Manhole covers
- Mehndi patterns (Indian henna designs)
- Mosaics
- Pets (e.g., cat and dog fur patterns)
- Quilting patterns
- Rugs
- Scarves
- Sculptures
- Shadows
- Shells (e.g., ocean creatures, turtles, and insects)
- Silverware
- Slotted spoons
- Stained glass windows
- Stitching, crochet and knitting patterns, yarn, ribbons
- Stonework, bricks
- Tablecloths
- Tattoos
- Tessellations
- Textiles
- Ties, suspenders, tie clips, cufflinks
- Tile (bathroom, kitchen, restaurant)
- Tread on the bottom of shoes or on tires
- Vases, impressionistic art, antique art
- Wagon wheels
- Wall textures
- Wood grain, woodwork (sculpture in restaurants)

Pattern Library

Use the following pages to seek inspiration and record new patterns you find along the way.

TEAR
PLAY ——→
OUT

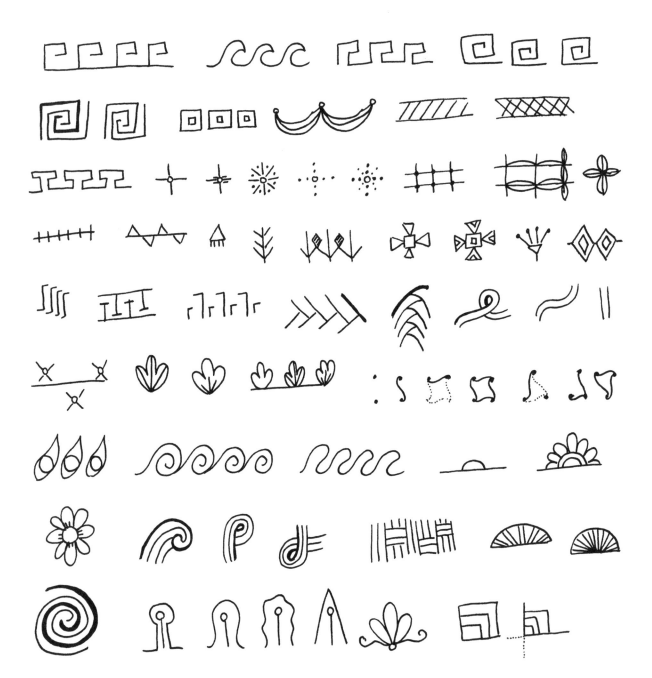

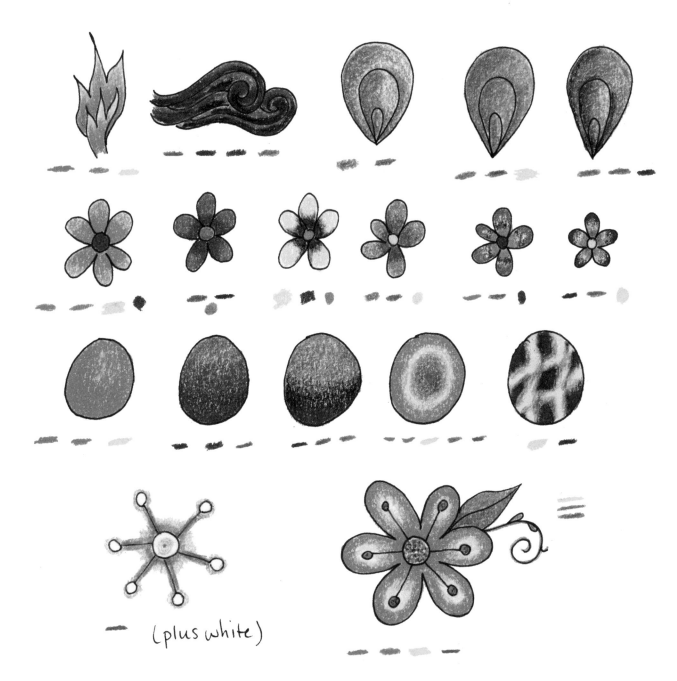

(plus white)

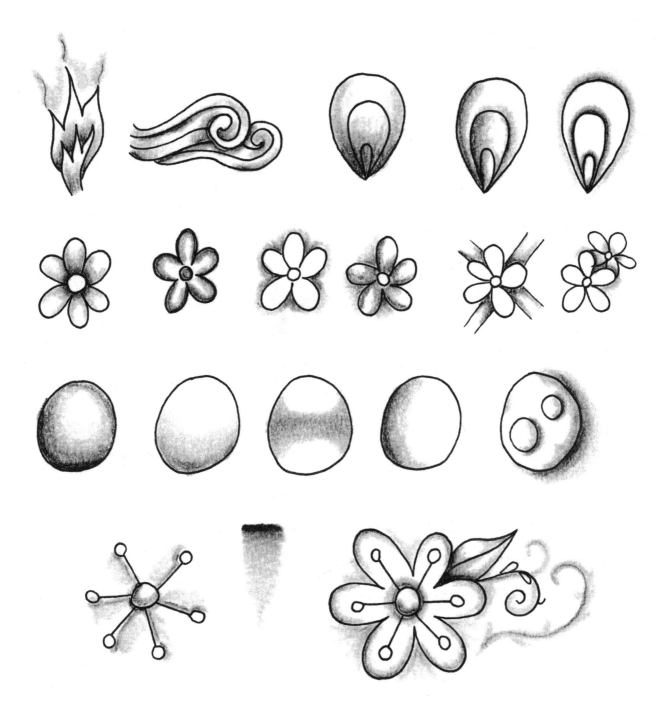

About the Author

Cher Kaufmann, inspirational art instructor and author and artist of *The Artful Mandala Coloring Book* and *The Ancient Alchemy Coloring Book*, holds public groups, professional presentations, and private classes on meditative drawing and mindful coloring. Through patterns found in all aspects of life and nature, she strives to open her students to worldviews brimming with awe and intrigue. She teaches the various ways to use pen and paper, as well as colored pencils and paper, but encourages any medium of art exploration (she especially loves photography).

In MEDITATIVE DRAWING workshops, Cher incorporates the ease of repetitive patterns in order to create focused stimulation for the mind and relaxation in the body, which allows mind and body to work together harmoniously. She supports her students as they begin to connect to the process of drawing and not just to draw.

MINDFUL COLORING workshops emphasize having fun as they also deepen the experience of coloring toward a truly calming state of being. She uses her art degrees and diverse range of studies (Face Reading, Ayurvedic arts, and pattern recognition in energy) to inspire others.

Cher is also a massage therapist and Reiki master, and has rigorous training in the Yuen Method and Matrix Energetics, as well as other healing modalities. She teaches students to ease tensions and initiate creativity through the combination of her unique education, using everyday practicality to guide others toward life-changing skills. She also instructs the ever-evolving perspective on nature and the influence of the five-element theory of Chinese medicine.

She hopes that her books will spark readers to flourish with balanced wholeness, that their curiosity continues with new eyes, and that they honor individual growth along the journey.

Cher's meditative art process provides the mind, body, and spirit with a small sanctuary, leaving her readers relaxed and rejuvenated, empowered and strong.

So in Cher's famous words: Smile, breathe, drink water, and have fun!